How to Be A Good Grandparent

Other Moody Press books by Stephen and Janet Bly:

Devotions with a Difference (for highschoolers)
Questions I'd Like to Ask (for 8- to 12-year-olds)
How to Be a Good Dad
How to Be a Good Mom
Be Your Mate's Best Friend

How to Be
A Good
Grandparent

by

Stephen
& Janet Bly

MOODY PRESS

CHICAGO

© 1990 by
STEPHEN AND JANET BLY

All Scripture quotations, unless noted otherwise, are from the *New American Standard Bible*, © 1960, 1962, 1963, 1968, 1971, 1972, 1973, 1975, and 1977 by The Lockman Foundation, and are used by permission.

ISBN: 0-8024-3577-7

1 2 3 4 5 6 7 8 Printing/GB/Year 94 93 92 91 90

Printed in the United States of America

To Zachary Nathaniel
and all of our
little Buckaroos & Buckarettes

Contents

1. "They Don't Make Grandmas and Grandpas
   Like That Anymore"   9
2. How to Make Them Feel Special—
   Without Taking Them to Disneyland   25
3. When Grandma and Grandpa Can't Agree   39
4. Long-Distance Grandparenting   53
5. How to Keep the Family History Alive   67
6. Teaching Your Grandchildren Your Unique Skills   81
7. Support Your Grandchildren's Parents   95
8. If Your Grandkids' Parents Divorce   109
9. Transmitting Spiritual Truth to Squirmy Little Kids   123
10. Teaching Proper Behavior Without Nagging   137
11. How to Spend a Vacation Together . . and Not Be Worn
    to a Frazzle   149
12. How Any Grandparent Can Be the World's Best
    Baby-sitter   161
13. How to Pray for Your Grandchildren   173
14. How to Be a Grandparent Your Grandkids Can Count On   185
    Index   193

Acknowledgments

Many thanks to all of our special friends . . .
grandparents . . . parents . . . and children . . .
who contributed their experiences to the making of this book

1

"They Don't Make Grandmas and Grandpas Like That Anymore"

The last terrific grandmas died just before the war.

Well, not exactly.

But there does seem to be an idea that grandparents of a previous generation captured a special quality that is hard to duplicate in our day. That's not true—but grandparenting has changed some.

In those "olden days," grandparents were general practitioners. Grandpa could shoe a horse, crank a Model-T, build a barn, plumb the house, catch the biggest lunker in the lake, and discuss world politics—all in the same week. Grandma could fashion a formal for her daughter, put up four dozen quarts of peaches, help the milk cow deliver a calf, tack up a starburst quilt, whip up a batch of fudge, and sing all the words of the "Hit Parade's" top ten songs—all in the same day.

Nowadays we tend to specialize. Grandads are vice-presidents of something, or they're the line supervisor, or they own a mini-mart. Grandmas are busy selling real estate, or running the dress shop, or taking a case to court.

But that reflects a change in society, not in grandparents. Even in the highly technical, mobile, and increasingly impersonal gathering we call modern society, there are some really great grandparents.

And there are a lot more who would like to be. That's where a book like this can be most useful.

You and I grew up in a very different world than our grandkids. Yesterday's models, and yesterday's ideas, don't always translate straight across today. Steve grew up, for instance, with one set of grandparents living across the street, and the other set two doors down. Today you're lucky to be within an hour of your grandkids.

However, the importance of grandparents in the life of children hasn't changed. That's why we all need to continue to work to be the best grandparents possible.

One of the great delights of grandparenting comes when you realize you're not the parent. Grandparents are expected to be different.

We surveyed dozens of kids with the question, "How are grandmas different from mothers?" and, "How are grandfathers different from fathers?" The answers tell the story.

Grandmas . . . always give you things
hug too much
like for you to eat a lot
accept me just like I am and never ask, "Why in the world did you do that?"
are harder to explain things to
like to smooch
say things like "A few cookies before dinner won't hurt anyone"
believe that I can grow up to be anything I want to be

Grandpas . . . have better stories than dads
laugh more
get sicker than fathers
don't get so embarrassed when you do something silly
need more naps
let you do things fathers say you aren't old enough to do

can tell you what you ought to do without it sounding like a lecture
know how to say "I love you" with their eyes
think that you are the greatest kid in the world when everybody knows that you aren't

Just how important is this role of grandparenting? Very important. Yes, Mom and Dad can do many of the same jobs grandparents can, but grandparents are especially good at certain, special tasks.

GRANDPARENTS CAN GIVE THEIR GRANDKIDS . . .

FAMILY CULTURE

Sure, Mom and Dad can take time to explain the family ethnic, geographic, or regional heritage, but it can sometimes sound like a parents versus kids conflict.

Junior says: "Gee whiz, Mom. Nobody in my class goes to the cemetery on Memorial Day. Everybody goes to the beach."

Mom replies: "We're going with Grandma and Grandpa. Grandma's only brother was killed in World War II, and your Uncle Bob, whom you never knew, was shot down in Viet Nam. It's our way of saying, 'Thanks. We haven't forgotten.'"

Junior says: "But, Mother . . . "

Mom replies: "Sorry, kiddo, that's the kind of family we are."

Two good examples (your parents and your grandparents) make a pattern, not just an alternative. In order to project a clear direction for the future generation, we need more than one reference point from the past. Parents can provide one of those points. Grandparents can provide the other.

FAMILY SECURITY

It's a great big world that, at times, seems to be out to make life miserable for a kid. On this sea of hostility, the child's home is viewed as a safe haven. But that's still a lonely world. One little isolated speck of safety on a big planet? But then there's grandma and grandpa's house. That doubles the security. With two sets of grandparents, the feeling is tripled.

A friend of ours reported, "One time I got lost in a big department store. I just knew that my mom had gone home without me. Since she would still be on the freeway going home, I called my grandmother. She talked to me for a long time, and then my mother walked by looking for me. I was so happy to see my mom I just hung up on Grandma. I'm not sure what I expected her to do, since I lived in San Diego and she lived in Houston."

Sometimes you need to have more than one source of stability and security.

A SENSE OF HISTORY

Raising, supporting, taking care of a family often demands so much from a parent there's no time to slow down and look at the past. Grandparents add depth, and therefore more meaning, to the child's world.

Parents might mention names like Kennedy, Mao Tse-Tung, and Elvis, but grandparents talk about the Roosevelts, Stalin, and Glenn Miller.

Sure, Dad once saw Stan Musial hit a triple and then steal home, but Grandad witnessed Babe Ruth rip one over the center field wall.

Mom remembers when Queen Elizabeth married, but Grandmother was there, glued to the radio, when Edward VIII abdicated.

Dad just might remember life before spaceships. But Grandpa can tell you about life before television.

Good grandparents are the living bridge between the facts of history books and the reality of today.

A SECOND OPINION

Confidential friends are hard to find. Sometimes you need a person to talk to who's on your side. You want someone to listen to the whole story. In a strong family, you'll find Mom and Dad ready to listen. But, every once in a while, you need a little more. A little doubt creeps into the child's mind about whether Mom or Dad really understood what you said. That's where Grandma or Grandpa can lend another ear.

Missy stops by Grandma and Grandpa's for a chat. "Mom says I ought to wait two more years before I get my ears pierced. What do you think, Grandma?"

Grandma smiles, "Well, honey, the cute way you've been wearing your hair hides your ears anyway."

Grandpa laughs and adds, "Missy, you've got to take it easy on the boys. You're so cute now, they're all heartsick."

"You really think so, Grandpa?" she searches.

"Honey, you remind me of the first time I saw your grandmother. She was about your age. I was up on a ladder stocking a shelf, when she and her father walked into the store. I thought I was going to fall off the ladder. So, you take it easy on the fellas."

"Oh, Grandpa . . . " Missy laughs.

But she leaves with a second opinion about the necessity of having pierced ears.

A BIGGER AUDIENCE

Everyone likes playing to a packed house. It's great to do your best in front of lots of folks. It's also scary. It doesn't matter if it's the preschool Valentine program, the piano recital, or the graduation speech—there's always the possibility of doing something wrong. So you look out at the crowd. There are some who will be the first to stand and cheer when you do well, and they will also love you even if you flop.

Look out there. Do you see Mom and Dad? Oh, wow, look again. There's Grandma and Grandpa. I didn't know they were going to be here. OK, here goes. . . .

LIFE'S EXTRAS

Sure there are some parents who can afford to buy their kids everything. We just don't know of many, that's all. So along comes Grandma and Grandpa. They've stabilized their income, purchased all the "things" they need in life, and cut expenses pretty well. So they saved up a little extra for emergencies.

You know, those critical things in life, like a new formal for Missy to wear to the Senior Reception. Or a "no interest" loan to Junior for a new transmission for his car. Then there's the green folding money tucked into the letter to the kids with a note attached. "Buy a little something extra for the kids. It's Grandma's treat."

SOMEONE WHO CAN HELP THEM SEE THEIR PARENTS AS HUMAN

There are times when every child begins to think that Mom and Dad were cut from another mold. Not only do they expect perfect behavior, but they seem to be able to set the picture of perfection themselves.

"I could never be like my mom. She's always so cool. She never gets excited and says dumb things like I do," Missy moans. Then she was at Grandma's one day.

"Did I ever tell you about the first time your mother decided to cook breakfast?" Grandma laughs. "She caught all the bacon grease in the frying pan on fire. So she grabbed the pan, still flaming, and ran out of the house down to the corner fire station yelling at the top of her voice, 'Fire! Fire!' She had the firemen put it out and then noticed that she was wearing only her shorty pajamas. She called us from the fire station, and your grandfather had to drive down one block, take her bathrobe, and then drive her back home. She wouldn't walk down the street for a month after that."

To which Missy replies, "My mother did that?"

Funny how grandparents keep parents human.

BRAGGING RIGHTS

There's little doubt that most kids are proud of their parents. From, "Well, my dad's a policeman" to "My mother's the president of the P.T.A.," kids can think of themselves as special because of the role their parents fulfill.

Grandparents can add to the child's arsenal of healthy pride. "My grandma brought me this from Florida" makes one feel like a seasoned traveler, even when attending the second grade in Chicago.

"My grandpa makes his own flies for fishing."

"You ought to see the lemon pie my grandmother makes. It's two feet tall—well, almost!"

Your accomplishments, skills, and experiences filter down to add depth even to your grandchildren's lives.

Kids need grandparents.

They need active grandparents.

They need grandparents who're not satisfied with watching them grow up from some far distant bleacher.

Active Grandparents	Passive Grandparents
call their grandkids	wait for the grandkids to call
know the grandkids' sizes	send a gift for the whole family
ask to babysit	babysit when asked
mark grandkids' special events on their calendar	read about the special events in a letter after they've happened
always have another trip to visit the distant grandkids planned	only see the grandkids when they stop by the house
display the latest school picture in their wallet somewhere	toss the latest school picture in a box
can name their grandchild's very best friend in the whole world	is not sure what grade their grandchild is in this year

Good grandparenting doesn't just happen. It takes some work. We've found five qualities common with grandparents who're serious about improving their grandparenting abilities.

GOOD GRANDPARENTS DEMONSTRATE
A SPIRITUAL DIMENSION

We want to be clear from the beginning. We find that grandparents who have a daily personal relationship with the Lord God have an advantage over all other grandparents. They have His help in that big job of grandparenting.

They have the wisdom of His Word, the conviction of His Spirit, and the security and protection of His power.

In addition, they have an eternal perspective on life that can greatly influence their grandchildren.

Can nonbelievers be good grandparents? Certainly. But there will be something missing. Without a spiritual dimension, life is never viewed in all its fullness.

For years we picked up copies of that classy magazine *Arizona Highway* and enjoyed the beautiful photographs of the Grand Canyon. Especially attractive to us were those shots of the colorful expanse of canyons with a sprinkling of fresh snow. Yet, even those professional photos could only show us two dimensions of the canyon. But, of course, we didn't know what we were missing.

Then, one January we drove to Arizona, turned north at Williams, and headed to the south rim of the Canyon. We arrived at the adjoining village late and checked into a motel. We set the alarm early so we could spend a full day at the canyon. The next morning we were greeted by six inches of fresh snow.

We entered the canyon right behind the snowplow and ahead of the tourist busses. We parked the car and hurried out on the point to experience the Grand Canyon winter. We gasped in awe. Suddenly, we shrank in size and got lost in the splendor of the sight before us.

Those tremendous photos in the magazine lacked a sense of depth and eternity that the canyon emits.

That's similar to the difference between spiritual and nonspiritual grandparents. The dimension of eternity is missing. Few children, of course, would ever complain about its not being there. They don't know what they're missing. But grandparents who keep a spiritual perspective as a vital part of their lives open a window for their grandchildren that allows them to catch a glimpse of all that life was meant to be.

Good Grandparents Have a Growing Faith

Remember all those chores we used to have as kids that the present generation knows nothing about? Maybe you were the one to gather the eggs, split the firewood, pump the cistern full of water, or chop the ice in the icebox. For most folks such activities are a thing of the past. They belong to another generation.

Grandparents whose faith consists of nothing more than a decision years ago tend to relegate Christianity to a past era. "Sure, religion was OK when Grandpa was a boy," some would say, "but it just doesn't fit us now."

On the other hand, a grandma and grandpa whose faith is an active, growing, daily experience demonstrate a vital spiritual life that is needed in every age and era.

A growing faith is one that is constantly learning new things about the Lord. It is a faith that does not know all the answers but knows where to find them. It's a life-style that seeks God's guidance daily.

It's fairly simple to test whether your faith is still in the growing stage. When your grandkids come over and the subject turns to religion, do you tell of events and experiences that happened in the past, or do you fill them with thoughts about what's happening in your spiritual life right now?

Good Grandparents Have an Adventuresome Spirit

There's great comfort in routine.

That's the very thing we work most of our life to achieve. Sure, things are hectic when we're young. We've got to work hard, take a couple jobs to make things meet. When the kids are little, they have demanding needs. We've got to push to get them through college, out of the house, and married . . . then we can settle down. But just as soon as we expect a peaceful, relaxed life, here come the grandkids.

We'd rather not upset our daily routine. You know . . .

"Don't bring the grandkids over between five and six because that's when Grandpa walks the dog."

"We'd love to on Thursday, but that's Grandma's club night."

"I know the grandkids would like to go to Disneyland, but I've stood in lines enough to last a lifetime already."

Good grandparents seem to be able to muster up the strength and the courage to plunge into something new.

"Mom, Mom! Guess what? Grandpa took me to a rodeo!" Missy blurts out.

Mom looks over the top of her glasses. "A what?"

"A rodeo . . . you know, with horses, and bucking bulls, and clowns, and men roping steers, and girls racing around the barrels, and everything!"

"Your grandpa never went to a rodeo in his life," replies the skeptical mom.

"Yeah, I know. But I wanted to go, and he said he had a 'hankerin' to mosey on down there' himself. Mom, what do 'hankerin' and 'mosey' mean?" Missy quizzes her mother.

We could tell Missy what it means. It means, young lady, you've got one good grandpa.

Good Grandparents Understand the Irreplaceable Part They Play in Their Grandchild's Life

Grandma is not a back-up mom. Grandpa is not a substitute father. There is a whole category in our hearts and lives especially for our very own grandma and grandpa.

Few parents need to be reminded how critical their place is in their child's life. They provide the food, clothing, shelter, education —everything.

Grandparents are crucial, also, to the child's life. But in a different way.

Good grandparents look at that list of things grandparents are especially good at providing, and they say, "I'm going to make sure my grandkids have all of that—and more."

Good grandparents look at the parents' busy schedule, look at the grandkids' activities, see all the many friends and close neighbors, and still realize that those kids need a grandma and a grandpa. So, vacation schedules are re-arranged, purchases are postponed, and the telephone bill shoots up higher.

There's no substitute. Without active grandparents there is just a void.

Good Grandparents Have a Willingness to Be Misunderstood

When Junior comes over to stay with "Grams" you end up at a department store sale and buy him a new winter jacket. But your daughter replies, "Didn't you think we could afford to keep our kids in warm clothes?"

You take your daughter's children with you on vacation—and your son complains that you didn't take his kids.

You call up and offer to baby-sit, and your daughter-in-law tells you they already have a capable baby-sitter, thank you.

Sure, things like that will happen from time to time. Let's face it, there will be times when you blow it. You'll say things that should not be said, or allow privileges that should not have been allowed, or show up at the wrong time. But the only sure way to keep from being misunderstood is to completely ignore your grandkids. Neither you, nor they, can afford that.

Scripture Foundation for Good Grandparents

OK, you say, we're going to set out to be the best grandparents possible. Logically, you open your Bible to see what the Word has to say. Then you discover that no one set passage describes the perfect grandparent. There is no equivalent to the Proverbs 31 verses for women or Paul's Ephesian 5 verses for husbands and wives.

However, the spiritual foundation passage for grandparents might just be Titus 2:2-5. It's Paul's declaration of behavior for senior citizens within God's family. Strengthen these areas, and you have the proper foundation for grandparenting.

BASIC ATTITUDES FOR GOOD GRANDFATHERS

"Older men are to be temperate, dignified, sensible, sound in faith, in love, in perseverance" (Titus 2:2).

Temperate	Sober. This means the opposite of overindulgence. By this time in a man's life he should have learned what are the genuine, lasting pleasures, and what is the phony,

temporary glitter. He knows, without question, that the slick pleasures the worldly system promotes aren't worth their cost.

Dignified

Serious. This doesn't mean stodgy, old-fashioned, or insensitive. It means you live out your daily life knowing that heaven is watching. It's the kind of behavior that inspires respect. It's behavior that encourages others to emulate. Dignity is that quality that rubs off on others, and thereby improves family life and community life. It is not a humorless attitude, but rather one that lives in the first glow of eternity.

Sensible

Prudent. This implies a man who has his mind under control. In the early years of discipleship there were struggles with your thought life, overwhelming youthful temptations, unbridled instincts. But you have been working on those. You have discovered the Lord's cleansing, His forgiveness, His deliverance. Second Corinthians 10:5 ("and we are taking every thought captive to the obedience of Christ"), which at one time was a distant goal, is now quite often a reality.

Sound in faith

Healthy faith. Your relationship with Christ has grown to a personal, daily, intimate conversation. The griefs and sorrows, the triumphs and joys of life have all taught you to trust God more and more. As a young Christian you were tossed around trying to understand the nature of God and the teaching of Scripture. Now you have found stability and assurance. Doctrine that at one time nearly floored you now sits warmly beside you like an old friend, bringing you comfort and companionship.

Sound in love A life filled with healthy love. One of the greatest dangers of growing older is to slip into bitterness, criticism, and fault finding. It should be just the opposite. Having seen so clearly our own faults, mistakes, and failures we should develop a great amount of sympathy and tolerance. Having experienced how little true, unselfish love is shown in the world, we should become centers of dispensing such love. God's patience and tender care for us, when we acted quite unlovely, should, by now, cause us to copy His behavior.

Sound in perseverance Fortitude. The years you have spent in active Christian life should have made you strong. The struggles, trials, tears, and victories have given you strength. Let the arrows fly, let the accusations come, let the temptations mount—you are ready to meet the challenge, you are in good spiritual shape. The body might grow weaker with age, but the spirit grows stronger. You're just too close to glory to back up now.

BASIC ATTITUDES FOR GOOD GRANDMOTHERS

"Older women likewise are to be reverent in their behavior, not malicious gossips, nor enslaved to much wine, teaching what is good, that they may encourage the young women" (Titus 2:3-4).

Reverent in behavior

A continual showing of love, respect, and awe of God. Not just reverent in speech, not just reverent while at church, but rather a life-style of actions based on the knowledge that the Lord is with us always. Such a person lives every day with Jesus as her companion. Every thought, action, and motive is brought to His attention, and His wishes affect every action.

Not malicious gossips

Before we get too hasty to agree with Paul and go on to the next quality, stop and consider why it is that Paul felt a necessity to add this warning. Obviously many senior women in Paul's day fell to this temptation. It still happens today, doesn't it? The lady stands in the front row at church and graphically "shares a prayer request" about her neighbor's immoral and despicable habits. Gossip is a game based on our own pride. It is our desire to be superior to others run rampant. Paul expects older women in the faith to be content with their place before the Lord and no longer have any use for the destructive tool of gossip.

Not enslaved to much wine

There are two obvious facets about this prohibition. First, it means don't drink very much, and don't ever get drunk. Second, it was obviously a problem among the older women in the church Paul addressed. Why would older women have such a problem? Probably the loneliness of being a widow, or the depressing thought that you aren't really needed anymore, or the boredom of living with another family where everything's done for you. Whatever the particulars, it was obviously a problem. Let's broaden Paul's words beyond the subject of alcohol and let them include prescription and illegal drugs, obsessive eating, and any other activity that produces a mindless, functionless stupor.

Teaching what is good

Paul views every older Christian lady as a teacher. Not, perhaps, in the classroom, but always teaching. The subject matter? All that is good. "Finally, brethren, whatever is true, whatever is honorable, whatever is right, whatever is pure, whatever is lovely, whatever is of good repute, if there is any excellence and if anything worthy of praise, let your mind dwell on these things" (Philippians 4:8). Who are the students? Mainly young women (Titus 2:4). Every day should be viewed as a teaching opportunity. Then allow the Lord to bring the pupils to you.

The whole passage in Titus reminds us that the family of God needs the counsel, service, and teaching of the older generation of believers. Your own family needs your wisdom and help as well.

Who are the perfect grandparents? We all have our imperfections, but one young friend of ours thinks his are pretty close:

> Grandma and Grandpa have a great big yard where I can do anything I want. I can jump in the leaves, build a fort, or make roads in the dirt.

I don't think Grandma plays many games with Grandpa, because every time I go over to their house, Grandpa stops what he is doing and wants to play with me.

Then Grandma goes into the kitchen and starts to cook us something. Not in the microwave either. She invents things herself, like my favorite double fudge oatmeal chewies.

Grandma has a great big fat book, and the pages are sort of worn out, but it has wonderful stories in it and she always reads me one or two (sometimes more). Then I get to sleep in a big bed and have the room all to myself.

I think my grandparents might possibly be the best in the whole wide world.

P.S. But Grandma does make me brush my teeth, and Grandpa made me eat some okra, once. Yuuck!

Letters like that, whether written on paper or written on the heart, make the last one-third of your life worthwhile. Being allowed to play a vital, special part in a whole new generation is a unique privilege. The task needs and demands good grandparenting.

THREE PROJECTS FOR GOOD GRANDPARENTS

1. Go to the phone right now and call the grandchildren whom you haven't seen or talked to in the longest time. Find out what they have been doing, and let them know you really love them. No matter how old they are, end the conversation with "I love you."

2. Take the next several days and write to your grandchildren one at a time. Among other things, tell them how you used to spend your days when you were their age. Write enough that they get a feel for life way back then.

3. Get another small purse- or pocket-sized address book. Compile the names, addresses, phone numbers (work numbers?), clothes sizes, hobbies, and favorite foods of all your grandchildren. If you have photos, glue them in also. This is your "grandkids' book," to be taken with you every time you go to the store, on a trip, or to a meeting.

2

How to Make Them Feel Special—
Without Taking Them to Disneyland

The pink dress in the showroom window had a price tag of $45. That's a lot of money to spend on a five year old who's growing out of her sizes every six months. Her mother told her that it just was not very practical and that the $16.95 pink dress on sale at the department store was just as nice.

Dad is tired of eating at the Burger Barn. The hamburgers are too greasy, the milk shakes too thin, and the fries taste like soybean paste. Sure, they have a nice playground, but he finally announced, "Millicent, we are not stopping there again!"

When Millicent asked if they could go to the movie *Peter Pan*, both Mom and Dad groaned. "The room's too dark." "The floor is too sticky." "There's too big a crowd." "The popcorn's too salty . . . and expensive." "We'll wait and rent the video."

Grandma and Grandpa Alberts stopped by last Saturday just to visit and ended up staying with Millicent while Mom got some shopping done. When Mom got home, there was just a note: "We went for a little ride—be home soon."

It was 7:15 p.m. when the tired trio barged in through the back door. Millicent was ecstatic.

"Mommy, Mommy! Me and Grandma and Grandpa really had fun. We went to see *Peter Pan*, and we got to have dinner at the Burger Barn, and guess what else? Grandma bought me that beautiful pink dress!"

At this point Millicent's mom turned to Grandma with the classic line, "Mother! How could you?"

How could she spoil her granddaughter?

Actually, it's quite simple.

And fun.

But, should grandparents spoil?

Yep.

Provided you understand and work within the limitations.

You see, to spoil someone is to give them better than they deserve. Every kid needs a glimpse of what this is all about. The Bible is crammed with accounts of how God grants us more than we deserve. Our sin deserves death—so what does God give us? "For the wages of sin is death, but the free gift of God is eternal life in Christ Jesus our Lord" (Romans 6:23).

So a sensible, reasonable spoiling might just help the grandkids understand how God can be so generous to all of us.

WHY DO MOST GRANDPARENTS WANT TO SPOIL THEIR GRANDKIDS?

It has to do with their relationship with their own grandparents.

There are seasons in life when the demands upon you are so hectic and crucial, there is no time to plan—only to react. A mom with a couple of preschoolers, for instance, has little time for relaxing in the recliner and thinking about past relationships.

But that's one of the benefits of grandparenting. Every now and then you get a moment to think about the past.

It was a really foggy morning, just south of Santa Cruz, California. Steve was spending the week of vacation with Grandma and Grandpa. Grandma woke him up saying, "Little brother, it's time for breakfast." That meant eggs, bacon, homemade biscuits, and gravy. Steve remembers Grandpa sitting at the table reading the newspaper, and over in the corner was the most delightful sight his seven-year-old eyes had ever seen. There were two fishing poles, a bucket, a thrilling, yet frightening, fish knife, and a box crammed with hooks, yarn, and little fake bug-like creatures of bright colors and wild designs!

Nothing had to be said, but he knew what was happening after breakfast. He and Grandpa were going fishing. They would drive down to where the waves crashed onto the sandy beach. Then they would climb those stairs to the top of the pier and walk those creaky wooden planks out over the thunderous explosion of surf. Somewhere, way out on the end, close to China, Grandpa would say, "Well, this looks like a good place to stop, doesn't it?" And they would spread out the gear and drop their lines. For the next several hours they would delight themselves by reeling in several dozen "Tom Cods" and by visiting about how things were in the "olden days."

Now when you relax in your easy chair and remember your own grandpa, you might have a different memory. But you'll have the same reaction. You'll walk into the kitchen and say to your wife, "You know, next time we stop by and visit the kids, I'm going to take Billy down to the river fishing."

"Oh, I don't think he has any fishing equipment," she says.

"Well, by george, I'm going to buy him some. A seven-year-old boy ought to have his own fishing gear. You know what I mean?"

She knows.

She knows you are about to spoil your grandson.

Now, some of you might insist, "I never knew my own grandparents, so how can thoughts about them influence me now?" But the very fact you did not have enough, or any, time with them pushes you to see that the same thing does not happen to the next generation.

Spoiling your grandkids has a lot to do with economic priorities.

Contrary to what most kids think, not all grandparents are rich. But somehow grandparents like to spend their money on things that grandkids like. That makes a nice arrangement.

What we spend our money on keeps changing over the years. Our Michael and his wife, Michelle, have this passion to buy a beautiful new car. They spend weekends at car dealers trying to find a great deal. Russ and his wife, Lois, scan the newspaper every week looking for the perfect house to purchase.

But things are different for us now. We have purchased our life-time home. Our car has 180,000 miles on it, and we aren't concerned about getting another yet. In looking around the house we realize that we will never have to buy another bedroom set, or another coffee table, or another set of silverware. Our clothes sizes don't change very much, and we have no compulsion to stay up with the current fads. Sure, we probably look a few years out of date, but that doesn't bother us anymore.

Most of the "things" we thought we had to have during the first twenty-five years or so of marriage, we have either managed to purchase, or live without. Besides, the closets are full, and the garage is stacked—we certainly don't need more.

It's also a curious phenomenon that for many occupations, you reach the highest pay scale about the time the kids are all grown and out of the house. So you end up with a little more time, a little more money, and few things that you need to purchase for yourselves. What a setup. Here we are, just ripe plums ready to be plucked by some of the cutest, brightest, most terrific kids in town.

"Sure I could buy myself another golf bag, but this old red jobber has followed me around the course for more than twenty-two years. Let's buy Junior that fancy skateboard he's been moaning about," we say.

Spoiling your grandkids sometimes has to do with their present environment.

Say your thirty-two-year-old son decides on a career change. It means two more years of school. So he plunges into the books, and his wife grabs the best job she can find. Somehow they manage to pay the bills, but that's about all. Meanwhile, Melinda, Marcy, and Martin have to cut back on some of the "extras" of life.

Then along comes Grandma and Grandpa.

"Grandpa says he'll drive us to camp!"

"Grandma's going to buy me the cheerleading outfit."

"Grandma and Grandpa said they would take all of us on vacation with them next summer!"

And there are some tough scenes that demand our spoiling attention as well. When the custody battle drags on, little Suzie needs to know there is one home that's not falling apart. When your son is laid up six weeks with surgery. When your daughter struggles through a complicated pregnancy.

Good grandparents know when to enter center stage—and when to exit.

When Anne started teaching art at the college every Tuesday and Thursday afternoons, her mother called. "Honey, can I swing by and pick up Sissy and Junior after school and have them stay with me?"

"Well, sure, Mom—if you insist," Anne stammered.

"Would it be an inconvenience if they had dinner with Dad and me on those nights?" her mother added.

"Oh . . . well, you know . . . if you insist," Anne's lips responded, but her heart was planning a quiet dinner with just her and Roger.

On May 21, the semester ended. It was also the last of the two afternoons-a-week stints for Grandma, at least until next September.

She knew when to enter—and when to exit.

The ability to spoil your grandkids also has something to do with the freedom you now have from the daily responsibility of raising children yourself.

It's interesting how that freedom changes one's view of things. You attend Sissy's fifth grade play and are simply delighted with her performance and how darling she looks in her "tree" costume. Afterward, you are free to go on and on about your little actress.

Mom sees a different scene. She has been forcing Sissy to sit still and practice those lines for more than two weeks. If she hears anyone say, "But, young lady, the dark forest is no place for a person such as you," one more time she'll scream.

And when Mom looks at the costume, what does she see? She sees three nights of working until midnight at the sewing machine only to be told after the costume was made that the one hundred tiny green leaves would have to be replaced with brown ones. She sees the pizza sauce stain on the trunk because Sissy insisted on wearing the costume at supper. She sees a little girl who pouted for a month because Melinda Mason was selected for the leading role, "even though everyone knows I'm better!"

Ah, the joys of not being Mother.

On Tuesday afternoons and Saturday mornings Junior's dad plays catch with him. That's a very good record. But Junior would like to play catch every night. At nine years old he doesn't understand things like yard work, paying the bills, committee meetings, and just plain exhaustion.

"Grandpa Powers plays ball with me every day he comes to see me!" Junior insists. "How come you don't play every day?"

Of course, Grandpa only makes it by a couple of times a month. But that's the joy of grandparenting—we might not be there all the time, but all the time we're there they can be the center of affection. We can spoil them because of the wisdom and thrill of living our lives closer to the finish line.

Now you might be a young grandparent at forty, or a more mature one at eighty-five—either way we're getting closer to glory every day. We've found the closer we get, the clearer the perspective on what's important in life.

Your son and daughter-in-law are extremely concerned because Sissy got a "D" on her report card. They have discussed limiting her activities, cutting back on time with her friends, changing her to another school, hiring a tutor, and appealing her grade to the school board. For over a week now, every time she comes home from school there is a barrage of questions about how she did in biology.

Grandma knows all about the trouble. But when Sissy stopped by last Wednesday not a word about grades was mentioned. There was the usual plate of warm oatmeal cookies and a kiss on the cheek with that bright lipstick of hers. Then the two ladies discussed whether they should go to the concert together on Saturday night or Sunday afternoon.

Grandma cares about Sissy's grades.

But she has learned that in the long run of life, one bad grade is not going to be all that important. Grandma cannot even remember what kind of grades her own children got in biology. At this point love and attention are extremely more important than momentary achievements or failures.

"Dad, nobody in this part of the country wears a hat like that! Why did you go out and buy Junior a $50 cowboy hat?"

"Son, I'm seventy-four years old. I've wanted to own and wear a hat like that for about sixty-nine years—well, I figure Junior just doesn't need to wait that long. Looks pretty good on him, don't you think?"

TREATING GRANDCHILDREN AS INDIVIDUALS

The Bible says we should "train up a child in the way he should go, even when he is old he will not depart from it" (Proverbs 22:6). This means help him become that unique person God created him to be. If our type of spoiling of the grandkids diverts them from this God-direction in life, then we have become a hindrance. On the other hand, if our spoiling action actually assists them in their God directed path, then we have neither brought harm to their maturity nor weakened their discipline.

But there is an important implication in that verse. "Train up a child in the way *he* should go." Each child has a different path laid before him by the Lord. Each child's path could be quite different from his parent's—or his grandparents. And it is almost certain each child's path is going to be different from his brother's or sister's.

That means, as good grandparents, we must treat each grandchild as a unique individual. Even though this sounds obvious and easy, two big obstacles often keep us from carrying this out.

First, it's easier to treat all grandkids identically. You only need figure out one response and then multiply it times the number of grandkids.

Here's the way we slip into that mold. You are vacationing in Colorado in November and find in a gift shop the most adorable red sweatshirts that have a cute, fuzzy teddy bear on the front. "Ah, hah! The perfect Christmas gift for the grandkids!" So you buy one for Anthony, Aaron, Abigail, Angela, and Arthur.

Oh, they all open their gifts with bright eyes on Christmas morning, and they will all write you a cute, scrawled thank you note, but two of the shirts will never be worn. You see, Anthony thinks he's too old for fuzzy teddy bears on his shirts, and Angela absolutely hates red. Sure you hit the mark on three out of five, but with a little more consideration you could have thrilled them all.

Second, treating each grandchild as an individual is not always understood by others. If you bought a bicycle for Jared when he was six, then Jamie expects you will buy her one on her sixth birthday as well. This might be a very good idea, or maybe not. It depends more on each child's maturity, interests, and personal circumstances than on their biological age. But grandkids won't understand all of this.

Their parents don't always understand either. "Mother, I don't know why you had to send Jason the box of candy and you didn't send any to Jessica." Well, Jessica had told you about being on a diet, and you hadn't planned on sending anything to either child. But then you heard about Jason's not making the baseball team and knew how crushed he would feel, so on impulse you sent the candy.

You were responding to an individual child's need, but it's not always understood. But don't let that stop you. It's wonderful what can be overlooked and soon forgotten because "that's just the way Grandma is."

Here are some ideas for helping you spoil your grandkids—in just the right way.

Spoiling Your Grandkids Good

CHANGE A FEW LITTLE HABITS

Yours, not mine. Make sure you single out each one as an individual. Next time you address a letter, instead of saying "Dear Rob, Ginny & Kids," try putting "Dear Rob, Ginny, Ralph, Richard, Rachael & Rebecca." Sure, it takes you a whole forty-five seconds to add the other names, but the effort is worth it.

Everyone, especially kids, loves to see his name in print and hear it being read. By doing this, you have grabbed their individual attention, even if just for a moment, and reminded them that there is a grandparent out there who cares.

In addition, you might try writing most of your personal letters to the grandkids. First, kids are thrilled to receive mail. They live in a world where there is no bad news in the mailbox. They never receive bills, pink slips, or threatening letters. The only thing they get are cards, presents, and occasional letters.

Second, you know their mom and dad will read the whole thing anyway. In fact, little Lester will probably read his letter out loud several times.

START ANOTHER RECIPE FILE

What? Another file? This might just be your most important one. Instead of A, B, C on the 3" x 5" index cards, list your grandchildren by name. Alton, Benchford, Clickory, and so on. Then begin to file recipes and food items each one particularly enjoys. Alton likes your taco casserole. Benchford won't eat cold carrots but likes them cooked. Clickory has to have ketchup on her hot dogs.

Now if you only have one grandchild, and a great memory, you might not need the file, but most of us need all the help we can get, and a little box of info like this can make Grandma and Grandpa seem like sheer geniuses.

The real secret is to review the list before the grandkids come over. You can plan your menus around some of their favorite dishes. We think grandparents have many opportunities to introduce new foods to their grandkids and should do so from time to time. But, it's not your job to get little Benchford to like broccoli. If he's demonstrated his disgust for the funny-looking green stuff, feed him corn instead.

One grandma we know goes to extremes in this area and has delightful results. Whenever the grandkids come over, Ruth prepares a separate meal for each of them. Charlie gets a hamburger and jo-jo potatoes. Cindy gets a shrimp salad. Gary is served pepperoni pizza, and Natalie has a peanut butter, raspberry jam, and banana sandwich on wheat bread.

We asked Ruth if it wasn't a big hassle cooking different things for each of the kids. "Because they live down South, my grandkids only get to come over to my house three, maybe four times a year," she stated. "Now here I am, alone in this big house, eating some little microwave dinner most of the year. I'm sure I don't cook four meals a week, so I figure bunching them up and pleasing the grandkids won't hurt me one bit."

Her daughter doesn't mind it either. "All the kids talk about for the two-hour drive to Mother's is 'What will Grammy Ruth cook for us tonight?'"

PLAN YOUR CALENDAR A YEAR IN ADVANCE

The amount of time you get to spend with your grandchildren depends upon several key elements. You have to take into consideration the number of miles between you, the total number of grandchildren, their ages, your health, and their parents' generosity in sharing their kids.

However, even in the most restricted cases, you will have a better time with the grandkids, and an easier chance to spoil them, if you plan in advance. So, take out your calendar and a sharp pencil, and start scribbling.

Here's the goal—you are going to spend personal impact time with each grandchild, individually, at some point in the next year. Personal impact time means that each of you walk away from the encounter knowing one another better and loving each other more.

It would be great if you could spend a week with each grandchild each year, but this is seldom possible. Here's one minimum goal you might aim for:

If you have:

1 to 5	grandchildren:	at least one weekend per year
6 to 12	grandchildren:	at least one day per year
13 to 25	grandchildren:	at least half a day per year
26+	grandchildren:	at least one evening per year

Now, some of you see the grandkids four hours a day, every day of the year. But that's an exception. It's rare to have all of them close by.

Remember, we said these times are for individual attention. Stopping by for the day and visiting Bob and Shirley and the kids doesn't count as personal impact time.

That's why you need your calendar. You've got to coordinate your time, and special days and events, with theirs. Here's what it might look like:

In June you are planning to go to an American Legion Convention in San Francisco. Your son, daughter-in-law, and two children live in San Jose, so you will spend some time with them. Now, Linda's thirteen, and Lisa's nine. You want to spend individual impact time with each of them. So you mark out your convention schedule, double-check with the girls and their mother, then plot your strategy.

On Friday, you will pick up just Linda at 2:00, drive back up to the city, and do some shopping along Fisherman's Wharf. Then, in

the evening, Grandma, Grandpa, and Linda will have dinner together at the Top of the Mark. You can stop by your convention ho-
tel room to dress up for the night.

On Saturday, Grandma, Grandpa, and little Lisa will leave home
about 9:00 A.M. and go into the city. You will spend the morning at
the zoo, the afternoon at the aquarium, and for lunch, you will sit in
the park eating hot dogs.

Sure, you will be spending more time with the whole family, but
in addition you now have some good plans for personal impact time.

Time to go on to some plans for the rest of the gang. How about
Travis? He's eleven now, and spends most of his time in a condo on
the north shore of Lake Michigan. This year swing by and pick him
up on your way to Cheyenne Frontier Days during the last week in
July. (Surely you *do* go to Frontier Days.) There will be horses, cow-
boys, Western art, parades, and carnivals. Of course it will wear you
out. But why are you saving up your energy, if it's not for the
grandkids?

Now, keep on working through the list. The activities need not be
complicated or expensive. Chances are little Charmungeon will love
a whole morning at the playground just having you sit on a bench.
"Watch me do this, Grandma! This is really neat!"

So you now have a Grandparent Calendar planned. Some of the
events will have to be switched around, but you've made some defi-
nite plans for the year, and the odds are good that you'll be able to
keep most of them.

MAKE A HABIT OF GIVING GIFTS FOR NO REASON AT ALL

Let's dispense with the obvious. You must have down all the birthdays, and you will remember to send a gift on time. (As well as one
for the holidays.)

OK, you knew that.

And they know that. In fact, it's so routine that it has almost lost
the sense of gift-giving. Kids think that they deserve a Christmas and
birthday present. Anything less would be child neglect.

So, how about reinventing gift giving? A completely surprise present for no apparent reason at all? First, set yourself a budget. Look at

the number of grandkids, the amount of income, and what would be a reasonable amount to use for such gifts.

Let's suppose you could afford $5 a month. And, for ease of planning, say you have twelve grandchildren. So, once a year, each grandchild will get a card that says, "I was thinking of you . . . " and a little present from Grandma and Grandpa. You don't have to make a special shopping trip because you aren't facing a deadline. But you just keep your eyes open for "Grandma and Grandpa" gifts. You might find one at the supermarket and another at the golf course. But soon, you will train yourself to be on the alert for such items.

If you want to add special delight, take the extra five minutes and wrap the gift in colorful paper and ribbon, and mail it to them (even if they live across the street).

Four year old Melodie marched into the preschool classroom carrying a $3 orange giraffe. During Share Time (it used to be called Show and Tell), she stands to show off her newest possession.

"My Grandma sent me this giraffe yesterday, and his name is Hubert."

"Is it your birthday?" a little friend asks.

"Nope."

"Well," he asked, "why did you get a present?"

Melodie sighed and shrugged her shoulders, "That's just the way grandmas are."

Smart kid. Smart grandma.

Now some of you are saying, "Most of my grandchildren are grown —what about them?"

Treat them just the same.

"But," you protest, "what can I buy a twenty-one-year-old grandson for $5?"

Car wax. Two bags of those miniature chocolate bars. Tennis balls. Ten pounds of popcorn. A coupon for two movie rentals at the video store. Remember, grown grandkids still need grandparents. Don't limit them because they're older, and don't limit them because they are richer.

The giving of surprise gifts can be a strong way of saying "I love you," and no grandchild on earth gets too much of that.

While you are at it, don't forget to spoil them spiritually as well.

In Genesis 48:9–49:28, elderly Jacob blesses his grandsons. Have you blessed your grandchildren?

There is a sense in which only God can bless. If blessing means to impart a spiritual benefit, then we all fall short. But blessing can also mean to acknowledge certain qualities, talents, and gifts in another (*Theological Wordbook of the Old Testament,* vol. 1 [Moody], s.v. *"bārak"* [p. 132]). So, a grandparent can thank and praise God publicly for those positive qualities in their grandchildren.

It might not be convenient to line up the whole crew and go one by one like a Santa Claus at the department store, but you can begin to look for opportunities to publicly make such a statement.

We suggest you do it at your granddaughter's twelfth birthday party, and your grandson's thirteenth. It is a transition time for kids, and a good time to make such a statement. If for some reason it is impossible for you to be there at the party, write down your feelings and have them read out loud. And, if you feel you just might not live to see your grandchild's twelfth or thirteenth birthdays, then do it when they are seven, or eight—or nine.

Those special words of praise, coming from the lips of a loving grandparent, for the whole world to hear, could just be the rock of character the child needs to hold on to during the turbulent teenage years.

Your grandkids need to be blessed.

So, spoil them a little—spiritually.

3

When Grandma and Grandpa Can't Agree

Adrienne flopped on the couch. "Grandpa, there's this neat program on television at nine. Since tomorrow's Saturday, can I stay up and watch it?"

Grandpa Thom paused from reading a book, looked over the top of his bifocals, and smiled. "Sure, honey, that would be fine."

Ten minutes later Grandma entered the room. "Adrienne, you better get your teeth brushed. It's bedtime, you know."

"Grandpa said I could stay up later."

"He what? When?"

"Oh, he just said it was all right to watch that special on television tonight."

Grandma cleared her throat and spoke loud enough for everyone in the room to hear, "And I promised your mother you'd go to bed early."

Her glare was strong enough to send Adrienne to her room and Grandpa scurrying for the sanctuary of his novel.

Oops. It looks like Grandma and Grandpa need some unity on their grandparenting.

Similar scenes happen all the time. Grandma hesitates to hand over the keys to her new Buick to her sixteen-year-old grandson, yet Grandpa says, "Let the boy drive!"

After repeated warnings little Adelaide still insists on playing with the scissors, this time cutting in two all of Grandpa's fishing lines. He rolls up a piece of newspaper and begins to give Adelaide a swat when Grandma's voice rolls out of the living room, "Don't you strike that child!"

WHY DO GRANDPARENTS DISAGREE?

First, there is always the danger of favoritism. Out of Warren's seven grandsons, only one likes to ride horses. Oh, the others are great boys. They come out to the ranch and ride the four-wheelers, or the snowmobiles. They will help feed the calves, pick huckleberries, and pat the horses on the nose. But Walter . . . oh, little Walter! He's been riding with Grandpa since he was three. Now, at eleven, he can ride every horse in Warren's string, including Star—who has allowed no one but Warren to ride him in more than fourteen years.

So, when it comes to setting down the rules, somehow Walter always gets an exemption. "Sorry, kids, Grandpa doesn't have room in the pickup to take you all to town today. Well, I do have room for one. Say, Walter—how about you coming with me?"

One vacation day Warren found Walter confined to his room. He checked with his wife.

"What did the boy do?"

"Oh," she said with a sigh, "he was up on the barn roof again trying to jump on the back of Snakey."

Suddenly Grandpa got upset. "Loretta, I've told you to let me discipline the boy. You've got all the other grandkids to keep in line, but I'll take care of Walter. Understand?"

Sure. Everybody understood that Walter was Grandpa's favorite.

In some ways, there will always be favorites. One grandchild will look more like Grandpa . . . or like the same activities . . . or remind him of his own childhood . . . or show some special spark of comradery.

Three quick ideas might help you deal with this:

- Don't call any grandchild your favorite publicly. Don't say it to him, nor to his parents, nor to the other grandchildren.

- Insist that all the grandchildren follow the same rules. Little Walter should never be allowed to get away with anything that his brothers can't.
- Explain to the others why you spend more time, or attention, with the one special grandchild. "Kids, I've got to go to town and get some paste wormer for the horses, and you guys know how crazy Walter is about horses, so I thought I'd take him along. Can I bring you a treat?"

Second, grandparents may disagree about how to treat the grandkids because of unresolved parenting. If the two of you didn't agree on how to raise the kids, you probably won't agree on how to raise the grandchildren either.

"Grandpa, do you like brussels sprouts?"

"I hate 'em."

"Me too. How come Grandma fixes them every week?"

"Oh, she read a long time ago that they supposedly keep you from getting a cold in the winter."

"I'd rather have a cold."

"Well, you can do what your mother always did. She would go back into the kitchen for seconds of meat and gravy and then scrape the sprouts into the garbage pail."

"Really? Can I do that?"

"Sure," Grandpa encourages.

In a few minutes Grandma strides back into the dining room. "Does anyone know how three brussels sprouts ended up in the trash can?"

"Grandpa said I could," Dennis admits.

"He what?"

There it is again, lack of a united view of grandparenting.

One suggestion to help remedy the problem is to take an evening (or a weekend) and discuss with your mate: "If we had it to do all over again—how would we raise our children?"

Make sure you talk about

> what you did right
> what you probably did wrong

how you might have handled it differently
the "one" thing we never could agree on
whether raising kids today requires different attitudes and
guidelines.

It's not a time to attack each other but rather a time to reflect. Grandparents have the opportunity to gain wisdom from the years of experience together. Careful, prayerful consideration of failures produces such wisdom. Refusing to face failures just produces bad habits.

If you really want to check out the details on a united view of parenting, you might enjoy chapters 5 and 6 of *Be Your Mate's Best Friend* (Stephen and Janet Bly [Moody, 1989]).

Third, some disagreements in grandparenting are nothing more than individual power plays. Very simply, Grams and Gramps aren't getting along too well, so each is trying to recruit the grandchildren to their cause.

Little things like, "Emory, don't go into the den after dinner. You know how grouchy your grandfather has been lately."

Actually, Emory didn't know Grandfather was grouchy at all. In fact, Grandfather didn't know he was grouchy either. But it just so happens that yesterday Grandma asked if they could go to Detroit next January to attend her cousin's daughter's wedding, and Grandfather said, "I'm not going to drive twelve hours through the snow for any wedding."

Thereby, Grandfather has been declared an old grouch. Things aren't likely to improve until Grams and Gramps get the trip to Detroit talked through. In the meantime, each one will tend to recruit children and grandchildren to his or her side of the debate.

Three ideas might help in a struggle like this:

- Solve differences quickly. Ephesians 4:26 says, "Do not let the sun go down on your anger." In other words, settle each disagreement on the very day it appears, never carrying one over to the next day. There will be a much less likelihood of grandchildren getting caught in the crossfire if things are settled quickly.
- When you are faced with a particularly obstinate mate, ask yourself, *In what way do I act the same way?* The truth is, the

longer you are married to someone, the more the two of you behave alike.

"I never act the way he does!" you claim.

Why do you say that?

"Because I always have good reason for the way I respond."

Could it be he has good reasons?

"Well, he never mentioned them."

Did you ask?

"No."

That would be a good place to start, wouldn't it?

So, Grandma went in and talked with Grandfather about the
trip to Detroit. It took him more than an hour of beating around
the bush to admit that he's been awfully worried about his eye-
sight lately. Things are blurry in the peripheral vision of his left
eye, but he's been scared to go for a checkup. Plus, he still remembers how they skidded across the intersection on the ice
last year, and he's a little nervous about the winter driving
season.

Suddenly, he's not a grouchy old man but rather a highly sensitive one about his slow driving reflexes and his declining
health.

- Commit yourself to building relationships with the grandkids as
  a team. Look for ways to present this image. Let grandpa's shop
  be as open to the kids as grandma's sewing room. Visit them together, rather than separately, as much as possible. Sign the letters, cards, and gifts from both of you (and make sure you both
  know what was sent).

Quit running for grandparent of the year. You're not the winner
because you have the most grandkids voting for you as their favorite.
You're a winner when the grandchild sees you and your mate in a
close, loving relationship.

Fourth, some grandparents have conflicts because of remarriages. "His"
grandkids get treated differently than "her" grandkids.

In chapter 8, we'll deal with the problems of grandparenting if
there is divorce and remarriage among your children. Right now,
let's stick to Grandma and Grandpa. If, because of your own remarriage you inherit new grandchildren, remember:

- It takes time to establish that special rapport. Few children can flip a switch and automatically think of you as a grandfather. You will more likely just be that old man who now lives with Grandma. (Or the old woman who lives with Grandpa.) Likewise, when your new mate looks at your little Lester, he won't see a lad who was born several weeks premature, battled to survive, was a full year behind his peers in size for the first seven years of his life, was constantly encouraged to eat more and more so that he would fill out, and now is an overweight junior high student with a very low self image and needs every compliment he can find. All your mate sees is "roly-poly little Lester." So, naturally, when you and your mate take Lester out to dinner there is a conflict on what you should allow him to order.
- It would be best if you take cues from your mate as to how to deal with the grandchildren. Let your mate set the style and tone of the relationship until you are well enough established to discuss the individual child's relationship.
- But the goal would still be that you treat both "his" and "her" grandchildren the same. This will take patience, sensitivity, and compromise.

When Edward married Irma he found out that she did not like having her grandchildren play in the formal living room. They all knew the rules, and when they went to Grammy's they headed for the den.

But Edward's grandkids were encouraged to make themselves at home in every room. The friction quickly appeared at the wedding reception held in their new home immediately after the service.

"We aren't going to let the grandchildren haul out the building blocks and spread them all over the living room—are we, darling?" Irma purred.

"My goodness, yes," Edward replied with a wide grin. "We certainly want them to feel wanted."

"Well," Irma cut him short, "I don't see how I'll keep our new house clean with toys scattered all over the room."

Edward stiffened, "We probably won't see the kids more than three or four times a year. What difference will a couple messy hours make?"

Whoa! Not a good way to spend a wedding reception.

What Edward and Irma need to do is sit down and go over the individual rules they have both been using with their own grandchildren. Wherever there is a conflict, then each side should report to the other the reasons behind their particular injunctions. If one side sounds more reasonable, admit it and change the rules with your grandkids.

Irma had made the rule about grandkids in the living room back when she lived on Fourth Street all those years. The living room, which was off to the north side of the house anyway, contained a cream-colored carpet that showed every footprint and smudge.

In Edward's former house, however, the main entry dumped into the living room, where he had always kept the television. He was used to the grandkids barging in and plopping down on the sofa.

It was time for new rules in a new relationship. Since the carpet was no longer cream colored, the grandkids were allowed in the living room. But all the games and toys should be kept in the den and limited to that room for playing.

Suddenly Edward and Irma felt compatible again, and both sets of grandchildren knew what to expect.

Many conflicts in grandparenting arise because Grandma and Grandpa have never sat down and talked together about the task at hand. Some people think that good relationships just happen.

From time to time you need to review all the grandkids' progress. It works quite well to do this as you drive along on a trip of any length. Just start with the oldest and work right on down. Review what they're doing, how they're maturing, and their current struggles.

Then ask yourselves, what can we do as grandparents to help them become all that God wants them to be? Toss out some ideas. Think of some creative answers.

Next, ask yourselves honestly, *Is there anything we are presently doing that might be a hindrance to their maturing?*

Be willing to change. The old adage "I'm too old to change now" is a lie. There is nobody on earth who's doomed to carry all his bad habits around the rest of his life. We can change, if we are motivated. And the needs of grandchildren should be the highest motivation of all.

Maybe it's time for the two of you to review the rules of your house. Or, just maybe, you will need to agree on some rules for the very first time.

RULES FOR OUR HOUSE

Grab a notebook, and jot down some answers to these crucial questions.

WHAT ARE THE RULES?

This can be a short list or a long one, depending on what the two of you think are important. The shorter the better. We begin to sound like a Pharisee when a list of dos and don'ts exceeds our age. Kids just can't remember everything. Remember God gave the Hebrew people only ten commandments, and even these proved difficult to obey.

The "Ten Commandments of Grandma and Grandpa's House" might be a goal for each of us. Most kids would relate best to no more rules than their age—that is, four year olds . . . with four main rules, and so on.

Also, make these rules the extremely important things. Most manners and customs can be taught as you go along without making a formal rule such as "wipe your feet," "don't slam the door," "brush your teeth after eating," and so on. So what are the important things? Each family will have their own. Here are some of ours:

Those dealing with spiritual matters:
- Every meal served in our home will begin with prayer.
- Any statements or inferences that dishonor the Lord, and His name, will not be tolerated.
- Every guest and family member is expected to attend worship services with Grandma and Grandpa.

Those dealing with relationships:

- All items in this home are for the enjoyment of any guests and will be properly shared.
- No one in our home is allowed to make derogatory remarks or comments about any other family member.
- Grandma and Grandpa's word is the final authority in all decisions in this home.

Those dealing with special conditions of our home:

- No one is allowed to go into the corral with the horses unless he first asks permission of Grandma or Grandpa.
- No one is to leave the boundary of our property without first telling Grandma or Grandpa where he is going and when he is going to return.
- Grandpa's hunting and fishing cabinet is off limits to everyone except Grandpa.

And then, there might be some general rules:

- There will be no alcohol, tobacco, or drugs used in our home at any time, by any person.

You work on your own set of rules, and then figure out how to state them in language that all the grandchildren (and children) will understand. For instance, the above rules could translate: 1. Always say grace. 2. Never cuss. 3. Always go to church.

Your rules will be unique to your needs. Maybe you have a sewing room that is off limits. Maybe you will want to insist on the type of music that is played on the stereo. Maybe you need rules to protect your goldfish. But make them short and essential.

WHAT ARE THE PUNISHMENTS FOR INFRACTIONS?

In order for any system of justice to work, everyone must know what happens when the rules are violated. Punishments should not be meant to get even with the rule breakers. They establish the seriousness of the rule and help offenders remember to be obedient.

Let's say little Jarvis—your cute eleven-year-old grandson—loses at a game of Monopoly and lets out with a string of expletives that would shock a truck driver. What is an appropriate punishment? No more games? Go to bed early? No dessert? A strict scolding? All of the above? It's something the two of you will have to decide.

Let's say Sadie, your pretty-as-a-picture thirteen-year-old granddaughter, goes out to the barn and rides your green broke three-year-old quarter horse without telling you. What should her punishment be? No more horse riding for the week? Not allowing her to go on the Saturday swim party at the river? No dessert tonight? Or what?

Obviously every system of justice works best when the punishment fits the crime. The more serious the infraction, the more severe the punishment.

It might be that punishments vary for different age groups of grandchildren. They might even vary for first offense compared to repeated infractions. The first time Junior leaves the barn door open and the horses get out might merit a reprimand, but any future failures a more strict response.

WHO ENFORCES THE RULES?

Who dishes out the punishment?

You could assign this to one of the grandparents. It's Grandpa's job, for instance. But this could lead to a good guy/bad guy kind of image.

One grandparent might be in charge of some rules whereas the other grandparent enforces others. For instance, Grandma's in charge of things that happen within the house, and Grandpa's in charge of the infractions outside the home.

Or you might just have a policy that whichever grandparent is nearest to the scene of the crime carries out the justice. When Sanford clobbers Lulu with a spinning top because she tried to grab it from him, there's little reason to wait for Grandpa to come home from the post office to settle the matter.

You could divide up the grandchildren. With Grandpa disciplining the boys, and Grandma the girls. Or Grandma the younger grandkids, and Grandpa the older ones.

Any way you decide could work, provided you both know and agree as to who's responsible. Of course your grandchildren, being not only beautiful and talented but perfect as well, will seldom need any correction. But just in case of some bad influence by ill-chosen friends, you will be prepared.

You could write to every family member sending along a handbook of dos and don'ts. But that might seem rather formal, even unfriendly.

Or you could post the rules in a small, framed chart and hang it in the hall next to the bathroom. But that probably wouldn't fit every household.

Perhaps it would be better to look for more natural opportunities to present the rules within specific situations.

Six-year-old Timmy comes over to spend a week with his grandparents. Every morning he loves to go fishing with Grandpa. And every morning Grandpa reminds him, "Timmy, don't get into my fishing cabinet. Those things are only for Grandpa to handle."

A week of such exhortation will remind Timmy of the rule about the cabinet for the rest of his life.

Also important is for you to share with each grandchild just why that particular rule is so important to you. You have to give them rules that make sense. "Timmy, don't ever use the Lord's name in a curse because He is my very good friend and my Savior. I believe that He is with us even now, though we can't see Him, and that some day I'm going to live forever in His home. I would be very embarrassed for Him to know someone in my home spoke of Him in such a disrespectful way."

A further fact to be remembered about your family rules: every family member is to obey them. Unless they have built-in age limitations, Grandma, Grandpa, Mom, and Dad are all required to keep the rules.

HOW ARE THE RULES TO BE AMENDED?

What if you made a mistake about a family rule? What if the circumstances have changed and the rule is no longer valid? Suppose your grandson (or your own son) comes to you and says, "This just isn't fair."

Chances are you have already made some changes in your rules, even though this might have been very informal. After watching your behavior with the grandchildren, your own children say things like, "You never let me do that when I was a kid."

Maybe some rules should change. If you've been on a personal crusade to stamp out rock and roll music—well, you've lost the battle. It's been around for thirty-five years and isn't showing any decline. Maybe you could let them listen to a little, provided the album cover isn't obscene. Your investment in a good set of headphones might be a wise expenditure.

Other rules will never change, no matter what the circumstances. God is honored and worshiped—now and forever—amen and amen. But this doesn't mean you refuse to even discuss the matter. If you have a grandchild struggling with his faith, discussion of this rule might be the very channel to sharing your own personal commitment.

WHAT ARE THE RULES INTENDED TO ACCOMPLISH?

If the two of you have decided upon a few rules, you now have a scribbled list on the table before you. So pick it up, and for each of the rules ask yourselves the question, "What is this specific rule going to accomplish?" Some might be intended to establish a God-fearing home. That's a very good motive. Some are safety rules, intended to prevent harm. Not a bad motive either. Some are designed to insure personal peace and tranquility. Now the motive gets a little fuzzy. When the rules absolutely prohibit a nine-year-old from acting like a nine-year-old they are approaching the severe and impossible category.

What if, for instance, rule number 34 states, "After the evening meal, all members of the household will proceed to the library where we will sit quietly and watch the evening news on television"—and you happen to have one grandson who is six and another who is eight? You're fooling yourself. Six-year-olds don't sit still for anything. Especially something as boring as an anchorman telling of the harvest of apples in South America.

Make sure your rules help them to be the best six- or eight-year-olds possible. But don't try to make them fifty-eight. Even the greatest of grandkids just can't do it.

DO YOUR RULES CONFORM TO THE RULES IN THEIR OWN HOUSE?

Most likely, they don't. That's all right. But you should make sure to discuss the difference. Wherever possible, it would be great to conform to what they are taught by their own parents. If the twelve-year-old is allowed to stay up a half hour later than the nine-year-old, you can easily accommodate that. If their mother insists that they have baths, and not showers, you can probably arrange that as well.

But there will be times where you can't compromise. "Well, my mother let's me watch soap operas on television," Sissy cries. You might just have to explain that rules at your house are a little different. Let them know that every home has its own rules, and that all houses do not have to be the same. But you can also lovingly insist that your rules be carried out in your home. Be ready to give the reasons to why you operate the way you do. No matter what the age of the grandchild, he is old enough to get a reasoned explanation.

At the same time, you've got to be careful not to sound judgmental about your grandchildren's parents. Just hug the grandkids, smile, and say, "Oh, your Grandma's just old fashioned. This is the way we do things at my house. When you have your own house, then you'll be able to set the rules."

Good grandparents agree on rules that are fair, reasonable, and open to review.

Grandkids can accept that.

4

Long-Distance Grandparenting

We hadn't visited with Chet and Rosanna for almost ten years. It was great to discover them at a conference in Michigan. After preliminary laughs, hugs, and chatter we got down to the important talk.

"How's the family? What are the kids doing now?"

Chet spoke up first. "Oh, they're all doing great! Matt and family are living in Houston. He's with NASA, you know. I always knew that kid was smart, but he's really something. He'll probably be managing director any year now. They have a big house out at Lake Jackson and three of the cutest girls in Texas."

Then it was Rosanna's turn. "You know our Bobby was in the Air Force? Well, he married a darling girl from Sweden. They live up in Connecticut on a beautiful old farm. He's still flying transport planes and enjoying raising horses and the twins, Terry and Tommy."

"How about Sandra? Did she make it through med school?" we asked.

"Oh, my, yes." Rosanna smiled. "Our Sandra! Can you believe it? She lives in southern California. She has a practice in Malibu and teaches at UCLA. She married Scott when he was still a quarterback for the Rams. He owns the cutest restaurant right on the ocean. She's expecting her second in February. We still haven't gotten to see Jeremy. But they're so busy. They never have a vacation. All the kids are such hard workers. I guess they get that from their dad."

"Wow!" we replied. "They have all really done well!"

"Maybe too well," Chet shrugged. "I mean, I'm really proud of them. But Texas, Connecticut, and California are a long way from Grand Rapids. We try to see them once a year, but it's getting harder and harder."

Rosanna sighed. "When we were younger, we used to make all these plans about what we would do with the grandchildren. But they are just so scattered. I wouldn't care if they plowed snow for the city, it would be great to have them all live a little closer."

"I wish the grandkids lived closer. . . . "

Bring up the subject of grandchildren with any group of grandparents and they all moan the same reply.

So, we reversed the process. We asked dozens of grandchildren, "If you could instantly change one thing about your relationship with your grandparents, what would it be?"

Ninety percent replied, "I'd have Grandma and Grandpa live closer, so we could spend more time together."

Then we investigated the other ten percent. They already lived near their grandparents!

Kids really want their grandparents close by.

But the economic reality of our day makes this a difficult task. In our area of the country, for instance, there are extremely few new job openings. The next generation has to scout out the big cities, and other states, to find employment that fits their financial needs. Of necessity, grandchildren wind up hundreds of miles away.

It might be worth the trouble for the grandparents to consider moving near the grandchildren. But many times, the parents are caught in a cycle of job changes and advancements that make their location a very temporary commitment. So Grandma and Grandpa stay put and watch the family drift farther and farther away.

How Can You Grow Closer to Your Grandkids When They Live So Far Away?

TRY A YEARLY SURVEY

This will obviously need to be adapted to the particular age of each child. But it is a good way to keep up with all the gang. One couple we know sends out a survey, a stamped, self-addressed return envelope, and $5 worth of McDonald's coupons each January, and they report a 100 percent reply.

A sample questionnaire for the six- to twelve-year-old set might be something like this:

1. Who is your very best friend in the whole wide world?
   Why do you like him/her best?
2. What are your favorite clothes to wear, and what do you like best about them?
3. What is your favorite game to play this year?
   Tell me the rules . . . how do you play it?
4. Have you been reading any in the Bible I gave you?
   Which is your favorite part? Why?
5. What's your favorite television show this year?
   What day is it on? What do you like about it most?
6. Do you ever get afraid? What scares you most? Why?
7. Who's your favorite hero, your favorite person this year?
   Why did you pick him/her?
8. If you could pick any job in the world to have when you grow up, what would it be?
   Why do you like that one?
9. Do you get lonely very often? What do you do when you get lonely?
10. What's your favorite color of clothes to wear this year?
    Do you have many things that color?

The secret to a good survey is to make it fairly short, adapt the questions to the particular child, and give a varied group of questions. Some can be ethical concerns, some spiritual concerns, and some just delving for particular preferences.

If your grandchild is committed to attending Sunday school, and if he has already made a personal decision for Christ, then you can use the survey to keep up on his spiritual progress.

You might ask, How's the Bible memory work going? What's the favorite verse you learned this year? What was the neatest spiritual lesson you learned at camp? What are the three most important things you'd like me to pray about?

Some of you might complain. "Well, we have thirty-two grandchildren; we can't possibly do that for all of them."

Why not?

Do you really have something more important to do than investing yourselves in the interests and opinions of your grandchildren?

TRY CONSISTENT LETTER WRITING

Let's be honest. Grandkids, whether they are five or fifteen or fifty, aren't very good letter writers. Oh, there will be an occasional surprise, but most often a scrawled two-line thank you at Christmas and birthday time is about the most any of us expect.

But that has no bearing on our ability to write to them. If you see your grandkids less than once a month, you should write to them often.

"Oh, my—such work!" you insist.

True, but they are worth it. You write to the power company, the telephone company, the book club, the cable TV company, the charge account company, the oil company, and quite a few others at least once a month. Surely grandkids are as valuable as bills.

How much time will that take?

How much time do you have?

Here's one plan:

1. Write to every *individual* grandchild.
   (No family cards or "To the kids" letters.)
2. Spend fifteen minutes on each letter.
3. Set aside the same time, every week, for letter writing.

Let's say you set aside two hours every Sunday afternoon. That means you can write to eight different grandkids each week. Or thirty-two in a month! If you only have four grandkids, write to one each week, and so on.

If writing is really hard work, then consider it a worthwhile job. What if, in order for your grandkids to complete their education, you needed to take on a two-hour-a-week part-time job? What if there were just no alternatives? Most of us would push ourselves to do it.

Well, that's exactly what a serious letter-writing campaign can accomplish. It can be a part of their education. And who's to say which is the most important?

What will you write about? Most times you'll find you have plenty to say. But if you need some help, here are twelve ideas that might get you thinking:

January—Share what your daily (and weekly) routine looks like—even it hasn't changed much over the years. If you are still working, tell them where you work, when you get there, where it is, what you do, when you get home, what your job accomplishes. If you are retired, chances are you are busier than ever. Tell them about the golf on Tuesdays, senior citizens volunteer work on Thursdays, how you are building book shelves for the den, shoveling snow, working at the hospital auxiliary, or whatever.

Tell them when you try to get to bed and how early you get up. Walk through a day, or week, and give them a running commentary of your activity.

Whenever the grandkids think of you, you want them to have more than just this vague notion of a lady or gentleman sitting in a rocking chair beside the fire.

February—How about a commentary on world news events? They have access to all the facts. They can read or watch TV and see what's happening in China, Russia, or around the nation. But what does all this mean? Don't worry, you don't have to be a political expert. Just report on what it means to you. For instance, when the headlines blare out about increasing freedoms in the USSR, tell them about that Russian family that lived on your block in the 1950s and some of the stories they used to tell about life under Stalin.

If it's an election year, tell them who you have decided to vote for, and why. (Yes, even if they are only seven.) Share with them a particular worry you might have about our country. Or share an example of joyous freedoms and privileges we enjoy.

March—Give them a yearly geography lesson about how things look in your part of the country. Tell them about melting snow, the green meadows, the tall mountains, the flat plains, the city parks. Share a vignette about what the land around your home used to be like in the old days, before it was so settled. Tell them, for instance, how Lake Michigan is similar to the ocean they live next to, or how it is different. Tell them one thing you like best about this season of the year.

Tell them about the trees, the flowers, the soil, the crops and gardens or whatever other features capture your eye at the time as being unique to your area.

April—Spiritual struggles and successes. Write at their level but share what you are learning from the Lord. They need to know that the Christian faith is a growing relationship. It's all right for them to find out that Grandma and Grandpa don't know everything yet. Tell them how the Lord has answered your prayers. Tell them about some verses that you just can't seem to understand yet. Tell them about the most exciting new spiritual truth you have discovered in the last month.

You don't need to preach. Even if your grandchild is being brought up in a nonspiritual family, he or she will be interested in what is happening to you personally. Share great testimonies you have heard, exciting projects that your church is a part of, and about the interesting Christians you have met.

This might be the place to share about some famous people who happen to be Christians. If little Billy loves baseball, tell him about the major league pitcher who is a preacher during the off-season. You might even have a clipping or two to send.

May—Tell them about some of your best memories from when you were their age. It could have been during those hard depression years or perhaps wartime years. They could have been the lean years or maybe the fat ones. Tell them about what your school was like. How much homework you had. About your very best friend way back then. About how you got to school, what happened if you were late, and what games you played at recess. Tell them what you wore to school, what you had for lunch, and who was the kid in school you were most envious of (and why).

Tell them which subjects you liked and which gave you the most difficult time. To the best of your memory, plunk them down beside you in that classroom and describe the whole scene. Help them to feel the hard wooden seat, fiddle with the ink well, and hear the screech of Clarence Nalley's fingernails across a blackboard that was actually black.

June—Send them a yearly survey you've filled out yourself. Take some of the same questions you asked them earlier. Tell them about your best friend, how the relationship came about, and what it means to you. Tell them about your favorite color for clothes, your most-watched television show, and your shoe size.

It would be a great idea when you send the yearly survey to ask your grandkids to make up their own survey and send it to you. If they do this, you have a ready-made topic for the next monthly letter. Some grandkids won't follow through, so send them the answers anyway.

July—Tell them all about a vacation you will never forget. Maybe it was the first time you saw the Pacific Ocean. (Remember how you rode for six days on the train to the West Coast and then ran right out with your good shoes still on and stood in the breakers? You know, things like that.)

Tell them what made the trip special. Maybe it was the people you were with, or the scenery, or the activities, or the people you met along the way, or just the season of your life at the time. Tell them about the wilderness camping trips you took because you were too poor for anything else or the time your rich uncle paid your way to Europe.

August—give them a good review about books that you've read and you think they will like. Here's a plan that helps your grandkids to enjoy reading. Go to the bookstore and ask the clerk which are the three most popular books currently selling for the age group of your grandchildren. Then glance through them and see if one seems better than the others. If so, then buy it. But don't mail it yet.

Read the book yourself, and if, indeed, it seems on target, then write to your grandchild and tell him all about how you enjoyed the book. Next month, send him the book, and ask him to tell you what parts he enjoyed most. There are very few statements more authoritative than, "Me and my grandma think this is a really good book."

September—Get reflective. Share with them why it is you are looking forward to heaven. It's a time to share some of those beautiful passages of Scripture about eternity. It's a time to give your philosophy of life about how to survive with the imperfection of this present world.

"Grandma always liked to talk about heaven."

It's a testimony that will outlive you. An outspoken atheistic friend once admitted in private that the one fact of Christianity that he could never come to terms with was his own grandmother's faith.

"All she ever talked about was heaven. On the very day she died, that's all she wanted to discuss. Even when she knew she only had a few hours left, she just smiled and said she could hardly wait. Every time I've convinced myself that God doesn't exist, Grandma's smile and final words come to my mind. I wish I didn't think of her so often!"

Never stop telling them about the Lord.

October—Ask them their advice. Find something that they are very interested in, and ask for their opinion.

For instance, suppose you are considering buying a new car. Poll all your grandkids and find out what kind and color they think you ought to get. Tell them you want to find a fuel efficient four door that's fun to drive—if that's your style. Or tell them you're leaning toward a 4 x 4 pickup with stick shift . . . whatever you want. Even your seven-year-old grandson will have some opinion. "Get a black one!" he pleads. Your twelve year old might try to convince you how you really need a Trans-Am, and your sixteen-year-old granddaughter just knows you'll be happy with a red Corvette convertible!

They will all have fun giving Grandpa and Grandma their opinions. Then, when you make the purchase, write back to all of them and tell them why you decided on this one.

You might ask them what kind of stereo to buy, or which science video they would recommend you purchase, or which pizza place is the best, or which is the best television show to watch on Saturday nights.

Cultivate opportunities for them to give you a little friendly counsel. And listen to their replies. Kids have a habit of sometimes being right!

November—Share with them what you are thankful for this year. This is especially crucial if you will not be with them on Thanksgiving Day. Be sure to give the Lord the thanks and honor. Jot down a quick review of all the times He has supplied just what you needed. Walk through your calendar month by month, touching on those special blessings and the tough times He saw you through.

Let them know how thankful you are to the Lord for each of them being a part of your life. Let them know about your delight in their friendship. And share with them what you will be doing on Thanksgiving Day.

Maybe for you there will be a "Thanksgiving Day I'll never forget!" story to share. You might not be there in person to insure that they pause and turn their thoughts to the Lord, but your letter can do the job in your absence.

December—Get theological. Talk about the joyous fact that God became "flesh, and dwelt among us" (John 1:14). Explain the glory and splendor of the first Christmas morning. Let them know how important it is that the Savior who died for us was no other than "'Immanuel,' which translated means, 'God with us'" (Matthew 1:23).

You don't need to take time to deride the commercialization of Christmas or the secularization of all the images. Remember it is a glorious, thrilling holiday to kids. Build from that foundation and tell them why it is so wonderful. Explain about the generosity of our heavenly Father. Take the symbols of Christmas and teach some spiritual truth. Angels . . . with the shepherds. Star . . . over Bethlehem. Gifts . . . like the wise men brought. Splash of colorful lights . . . reminding us of the great joy of the event.

Now you're getting the idea.

There are plenty of things to write about.

Just remember a separate letter and envelope to each grandchild.

A few years ago Janet taught a weekday class of fifth- and sixth-grade girls. About once a month they would have a special event, and Jan would send a note to each girl describing the event.

One week, after the letters went out, a girl named Jody came running into class with a wide smile splashed across her freckled face.

"Mrs. Bly, your letter was the first mail I ever got in my whole life!"

She was twelve years old.

No mail?

She must have lost her grandparents at an early age.

TRY MEANINGFUL TELEPHONE CALLS

Letters are great, but they can't draw you quite as close as actually hearing a voice. But how can you do that without going broke?

Do the obvious. Find out when the best long-distance phone rates are. Maybe it's in the evenings, early mornings, or weekends.

If you can, take advantage of time differentials. If you get up on the Pacific coast at 6:00 and call the grandkids in Ohio, it's 9:00 A.M. there. You get the best rate without stirring them out of bed before daylight.

Check with your phone company ahead of time and find out exactly what a three-minute call to each of your grandchildren will cost. Keep that information near your telephone directory. Then you won't have any surprises on the next telephone bill.

How do you make calls meaningful?

- Plan out what you are going to ask ahead of time. Don't call up, and then search for something you want to say. Jot down a note or two, because it will be easy to forget.
- Don't ask the obvious. If it's the middle of winter and they live in Alaska, don't ask if it's cold.
- Try not to ask too many questions that can be answered "yes" or "no." "Did you have a good day at school today?" will get a

short, uninformative answer. But, "What was the most fun thing you did at school today?" will often get a more interesting reply.

- Tell them, every time, that you miss them and you love them. They need to hear from your lips and in your voice that you really care for them. Don't ever think they have outgrown it.

Most times, to save money, talks to the grandkids will be pigtailed at the end of conversations with their parents. If so, then try to have time to speak to each of the kids separately.

If you can at all afford it, call up the grandkids on their own. Say, on Tuesday, call and talk to Jake. On Wednesday, Sarah. And on Thursday, Emily. You don't need to talk to the son and daughter-in-law—just the kids.

"Grandma called me last night," little Charlie reported.

"Just to talk to you?"

"Yep."

"Well, what did she want?"

"She wanted to know if I thought the Cubs could hold on and win the pennant. I told her if they don't get some help at the plate they would fold by Labor Day." Charlie shrugged.

"What did your grandma say?"

"Oh, she just said she loved me and would call me after the first of September. I've always got to explain baseball to her," Charlie reported. "Sometimes my grandma needs me to help her."

Smart kid.

Smart grandma.

TRY MODERN TECHNOLOGY

Now that we've exhorted you in the area of letter writing and phone calls, let's back up and rearrange the schedule. Instead of writing every month, you might be able to do something a little different to communicate with your grandchild.

Almost every home in our country has some type of cassette tape player. It's hard to imagine any modern kid that doesn't have at least one system in his room. Most automobiles come equipped with them.

You might want to make a tape and send it to your grandchild. It certainly takes less time than writing and, once the equipment is purchased, costs less than a long-distance phone call. Tapes are especially valuable for grandkids who live in an area where you can't often call—such as if their folks are on a mission station in Africa.

A small cassette recorder with a built-in microphone is a simple tool to operate. You just push on the "record" button, talk into the mike, punch the "off" button, insert the tape into a mailer, and send it out.

Rules for making a good tape:

- Decide ahead of time what you want to say. Jot down a few notes so you don't forget anything.
- Relax, and try to set a conversational tone just as if they were sitting in your living room. You aren't giving a formal speech —just visiting.
- Reduce as much background noise as possible. You want them to hear what you say, not the radio or television.
- Ask several questions that will encourage them to send a reply.
- You might try using a theme, such as the ones we suggested for letter writing.
- Send them a self-addressed, stamped mailer so that they might put their response on the back of the tape and send it back to you.

Now, if you have the technology around, get brave and send them a video tape. Purchase a video camera and tape a little session so that they can remember what you look like. You can cover the same things as you did on the audio tape, but now they get to see your house—and you.

You can walk outside with the camera and show them the changing seasons, send them a short clip from your latest vacation, or show them what the neighbor's new sheep looks like. You can even shoot some footage down the hall and show them where you hung that little plaster of paris handprint they sent you at Christmas.

Video cameras are getting easier to operate, and many of America's homes have them, so don't neglect this opportunity to do some long-distance grandparenting. If you don't possess a camera, you might consider borrowing one from a friend or renting one for special occasions.

Just why is it that we all have cameras around that are so seldom used? Everything you can do with a video camera, you can do with a regular one.

At least four times a year, grab a role of film, dust off the old Instamatic—or Polaroid®—or Nikkon®—and shoot a roll for the grandkids. Show them the new dog, the rebuilt garage, the tulip bed, the quilt in the guest room, and the snow on the roof. Most of all, show them Grandma and Grandpa. If you run a roll of twenty-four and only get twelve good pictures, that's still enough to send one to most all the grandkids.

You don't have to be the world's best photographer, just get them in focus and with sufficient light. Most modern cameras do that for you. Lots of supermarkets have a double print special where you can get two of every shot for the same price as one, and thereby save some bucks. Watch for their film sales and developing specials. It won't be all that expensive.

You might want to encourage the grandkids to take pictures as well. Buy them a simple camera, if you need to. Then once every few months send them a roll of film and return postage to mail it back to you when they are through. Then you take it to the market and get it developed. If you get double prints, you can send them a set of their fine photography and keep one for yourself. It makes a delightful telephone conversation to have them go through the shots explaining each one in detail to you.

We have never, ever, met anyone who complained about having too many pictures of their grandparents. The common woe is just the opposite.

Grandkids.

When the Lord said, "Be fruitful and multiply, and fill the earth, and subdue it" (Genesis 1:28), some families seem to be taking on the whole burden themselves.

You might have grandkids scattered all over the country and the world.

You might have some that are old enough to have their own children, and others still in the crib.

They might be actors or doctors, politicians or pilots.

Some of them could be well over six feet tall, and others less than one hundred pounds soaking wet.

But all of them have two things in common.

They're related to you.

And they need an active grandma and grandpa.

Don't let distance rob them—or you—of this pleasure.

5

How to Keep the Family History Alive

In the spring of 1869 Thomas "Bronc" Barstow helped drive 3,600 head of cattle from the Rio Grande River in Texas to the railhead in Kansas. After collecting his pay, he rode on to Omaha, Nebraska, and boarded one of the first intercontinental trains west. He left the train at Ogden, Utah, and worked his way north.

By 1875 Bronc operated a livery stable in Bozeman, Montana Territory. It was there he met Katherine Sample, formerly of Boston, Massachusetts, and the two married. During the 1880s they ran a cattle spread in the Teton Valley of eastern Idaho Territory. Eleven children were born to them, but only nine survived infancy. By 1890 the cattle ranch, like many around them, had gone broke.

The Barstows moved to Spokane, Washington, in the early '90s and ran a feed store, but when the Nez Percé reservation opened up for partial white settlement in 1896, Bronc and Katherine staked out a claim and moved to the Camas Prairie.

The B-B Ranch has been in business ever since.

Now, this is all a nice little story. But it won't mean a whole lot to you. The Barstows are not a famous family. You've never heard of them, unless you're a very old-timer around Lewiston, Idaho, and remember when Kenny Barstow shot out all the street lights along Main Street one New Year's Eve.

But all of this is extremely important to Lorraine Barstow McDonald. Last winter, while sorting through an old trunk of personal belongings left in her grandmother's estate, Lorraine ran across the diary of Katherine Sample Barstow, her grandmother's grandmother.

"I cried when I read it," Lorraine admitted. "The words, phrases, expressions, actions—they were all so classically Barstow. We haven't changed a whole lot in a hundred years. When she wrote about the pain and sorrow of losing little Susan in the flood of '89 I just broke down and sobbed. I mean, it's my family. Those are my kin! Suddenly, I felt very much aware of my place in history. I felt the necessity to carry on tradition. I went right out and bought a journal. My great-great-grandkids should have the same strengths that I received."

Lorraine is one of the lucky ones.

Most of us have only a glimpse of our family's past. If we were fortunate, perhaps we can remember a few of the stories that our grandparents used to tell. But that's about it. It's as if the Lord created each family brand new without any connection to the past.

But He didn't.

In fact, God thinks that it is extremely important to remember the former days.

"Only give heed to yourself and keep your soul diligently, lest you forget the things which your eyes have seen, and lest they depart from your heart all the days of your life; but make them known to your sons and your grandsons" (Deuteronomy 4:9).

The whole book of Deuteronomy could be entitled "Lest Thou Forget." God expects one generation to learn from the previous. He does not intend to have to reteach every lesson. And He is counting on that heritage to be passed down from family to family.

Why Grandparents Sometimes Fail to Chronicle Their Lives

You and I have two main enemies that prevent us from chronicling our lives for future generations.

First, we say, "Nothing interesting has ever happened to me."

OK, you didn't cross the desert in a covered wagon, lead the charge up San Juan Hill, serve in China with Lottie Moon, capture Pancho Villa, wade ashore with General MacArthur, shake hands with Humphrey Bogart, attend a conference with Eleanor Roosevelt, or step on the moon with Neal Armstrong. Your personal exploits never made the cover of *Life* or *Look*, and your family never modeled for a Norman Rockwell painting.

So your life story would never make a major motion picture or even a dime novel. But, you are exactly the one who needs to work at the transference of the family history.

There's an old, old story about a man from central Kentucky around the early 1800s who went off to seek his fortune in New York City. He had been gone for five or six years and had prospered as a merchant and trader. Then he decided to visit his old home area and friends.

As he got off the stage in Hardin County he spied a childhood chum. After some preliminary greetings, he quizzed his friend about what had happened in central Kentucky during his absence.

"Oh, Harvey, you know what it's like. Nothing new never happens here."

"Well, Matthew, surely something has happened. After all, I've been gone for over five years! Don't tell me everything's the same."

"Now what in the world significant could happen in this part of the country? It's just the same. I mean, this is the backwoods."

"Yeah, I guess you're right. Nothing ever happens. It's incredible."

"Oh, well . . . Mrs. Lincoln had a baby—but that's about it."

"A girl or a boy?"

"A boy . . . Arnold . . . or Abraham . . . or something like that."

Nothing happened?

One of the world's greatest leaders was born, but no one noticed it at the time.

Most times we will never have any historical perspective of our own times until we've had twenty-five years to look back on them. Our present young generation looks back on the 1950s with awe. They like the tunes and the cars from that era. But all of us sailed though the '50s thinking everything was peaceful and routine. Certainly nothing worth writing about.

We were wrong.

But let's speculate that you are right. Nothing eventful in the history of the world happens during your lifetime. You spend your entire life in a dull, boring, peaceful, contented rut.

So, you say, no one would want to read your journal.

Wrong again.

Little Sarah Anne—she's going to be your red-headed grand-daughter's granddaughter—will be thrilled to see what life was like in the twentieth century. She'll roll on the floor with laughter when you describe what your kitchen's like. She'll be thrilled beyond words to hear a description of tall forests and wildflower-covered hills. And she'll shed tears when you describe how you cried on the day your daddy died.

Second, we say, "I really don't know how to write very well."

Well, you might be right.

But what difference does that make?

Have you been pretending that you are perfect and have an image to uphold? A family journal, or history, does not have to be submitted to grammatical scrutiny. In fact, if you wrote everything in perfect English, it would be boring.

Why?

Because that's just not you.

What you want to do is write very conversationally, so that the reader learns about your personality from the way you express yourself, as well as by what you say. If you pronounce "creek" as "crick," then write it that way. If you ramble on and on with story after story when you talk, then write the same way. This is the joy of a personal journal—there is no bad form.

Here are the only three rules to remember.

Write *legibly.* Use the best handwriting you can muster with your particular skills and health. If you can type . . . do it. If you have access to a computer . . . use it. If it means slowing down a little as you write . . . slow down.

Use *quality products.* If at all possible, don't use a faint pencil on the back of a shopping bag. Ink fades over the years. The acids in cheap paper eat away at the text. Worn typewriter ribbons strain the eyes. Invest in a nicely bound blank journal or some quality rag content paper. You want the copy to look just as clear in 2095 as it does today.

Keep your journal protected. It's as valuable as anything you own. Toss it in your safe, or when one volume is completed, store it in the safety deposit box. We bought a fireproof file box on sale for less than $20. Treat it like the treasure it is.

Ideas for a Family Journal

OK, now you're hyped. You zip out to the bookstore and pick up a gold trimmed, leather bound, 320-page book of blank pages—now what?

If you are really stuck on what to do, here are a few suggestions.

MAKE A FAMILY TREE

In the front of the book begin to diagram a family tree. It might take several pages. In fact, it might take several *months.*

The best idea might be to take a big piece of poster board (about 24" x 36"), then, using a pencil that is easily erased, diagram the whole clan. Start with you and your mate and work down through the kids and then the grandkids. By each person print his entire given name, the date and place of his birth, and, if deceased, the date and place of his death.

On a separate piece of paper begin to compile all of their names, addresses, and phone numbers, at least the ones you have.

And so on with each child.

It would then look like the chart on the following page.

If your grandchildren are married, then add the spouse's full name, and so on, and proceed with any great-grandchildren.

Once you have all of this done, you are ready to back up and include your parents, your mate's parents, and your grandparents.

But where do you stop?

That will be a matter of individual decision.

We recommend that you trace things back at least to your grandparents. At that level you can say, "Grandpa had three brothers, Mark, Andrew, and Philip; and six sisters, Angela, Natalie, Sweetie (real name not known), Lilly, Beatrice (who died as an infant), and Gertrude."

Husband	Wife
born (b)	born (b)
location (l)	location (l)

date married (m)
location (l)

1st child — spouse	2d child — spouse	3d child — spouse
b. b.	b. b.	b. b.
l. l.	l. l.	l. l.
m.	m.	m.
l.	l.	l.

children:	*children:*	*children:*
name	name	name
b.	b.	b.
l.	l.	l.

But we also recommend you add to the family tree the names of all your brothers and sisters, your mate's brothers and sisters, and all of their children, if you can identify them. In case your family is not very close, this will help your grandchildren to identify their counterparts in other branches of the family tree.

If you happen to have other data about your family, include it. And, of course, if you are related to a historically important person, by all means trace them back for the whole family to enjoy.

When you're finished with the poster board, you are ready to transfer the information to a smaller sheet. Record in your journal not only the diagram but the current list of names and addresses as well. Even though your tribe might be the kind that moves often, this will be a record of where they are at the moment.

If you really want to have some fun, take the smaller copy of the family tree to an instant printer and make enough copies (on bright red or green paper, of course) to send in this year's Christmas card.

If you made any mistakes, some of the relatives will be sure to point it out. And you'll be surprised how happy the kids are to finally find out who is connected to whom.

OK, sure, you'll have some entanglements. There will be a divorce and remarriage, stepkids, half-sisters, and the like. But you are acting, in this instance, as a reporter, not a judge. All you need to do is record the facts. Chances are the more complicated your family tree becomes, the more helpful such a chart will be.

A second type of family tree we would like to suggest for your journal would be a spiritual family tree. It does not need to be as complete as the first. In chapter 9 we will discuss in detail how to transmit spiritual truth to your grandchildren. For now, just a few simple statements about the spiritual commitment of your various family members. You don't have to say anything about those with no commitment.

Your entry might be: Grandfather Snively, converted and baptized in Basque County, Texas, 1908. From 1915 to 1927 he served as a lay preacher in Methodist churches. Sunday school superintendent at Clinton Memorial Church from 1927 until his death in 1943.

Obviously, you don't know all there is about the spiritual life of each relative, but jot down what you do have. Any casual reader of Scriptures senses the importance of genealogies. For instance, after reading the inspiring book of Ruth, you find out in the last few verses that Naomi's grandson Obed just happens to be the grandfather of King David.

Little David did not "come out of nowhere" to slay Goliath and eventually become the great king. We know a good deal about the character of his great-grandmother Ruth and his great-great-grandmother Naomi.

You might believe you are the first confessing Christian in your clan, but if you dig back a little, you may find a faithful grandparent as well. We need to understand the big picture of what God is doing in our families, and pass that news on down to future generations.

The two of us were twenty-three years old, and the parents of two sons, before we came to know the Lord as Savior. We immediately let our whole extended family know of our commitment. Some were pleased. Some noncommittal. Some almost hostile. And, at least one, was ecstatic. Janet's Grandma Chester was openly thrilled with our decision.

About a year and a half after our conversion, we decided the Lord wanted us in full-time ministry. That would mean leaving the peace and security of the family ranch, five grueling years of university and seminary work, and then relocation to wherever the Lord wanted us.

Again, some of our relatives rejoiced, some yawned, and some were worried about us "going overboard with all this religion stuff."

But one relative had tears of gratitude and delight. For more than thirty years Grandma Chester had been praying that one of her children, or her grandchildren, would enter full-time Christian ministry. We knew nothing of her prayer but were thankful that she lived to see it answered. She kept repeating Simeon's words from Luke 2:29, "Now, Lord, Thou dost let Thy bond-servant depart in peace, according to Thy word."

Why did we decide on this particular vocation in life?

It had something to do with a grandma's prayers.

It would be a serious offense to rob a future generation of knowledge of their spiritual heritage.

WRITE DOWN STORIES OF WHAT HAPPENED IN THE "GOOD OLD DAYS"

Now that family tree's outlined. Next is the task of writing down some of the stories from the "good old days." You don't have to remember everything at once. That's the beauty of a journal. You aren't giving a detailed chronological study of your entire life. Just a few glimpses of how things were.

If you are really stumped for ideas, how about a sample scene from each decade of your life?

What were the 1920s like? Not a historical account. They can get that in the textbooks. But describe in detail one scene from the twenties that you think typifies the action. Remember that time the baseball team from Lemon Cove rode the train down on a Saturday to challenge the locals to a contest? Wasn't that the time Bert Hamilton belted the homer to tie the game in the eighth, but the ball bounced on the highway and into the back of a Model-A's rumble seat? It was then you discovered that it was the only ball in town, and the game had to be called a tie.

Remember how you went ahead with the supper on the grounds anyway, and for ten years afterward argued almost daily as to which team was really the best?

Those are the kinds of scenes to write about.

How about the '30s, and the steady stream of fellas at the back door looking for work, or a meal, or both? Why not write about that

Thanksgiving when that family of eight from western Nebraska stayed with you until their car got fixed, so you all shared that one big pot of boiled potatoes and turnips?

Write about the '40s. What were you doing when you heard the news of Pearl Harbor? Jot down how you felt when your neighbor, Harry, rushed into the house shouting the news. Detail public opinion in your town the next day. How did you personally respond? Did you volunteer for the army? Start a victory garden? Sign up for civil defense? Or just proceed as normal? How did your home community change during the war? Where were you on V-E day? Or V-J day? Describe your personal feeling when you read about the atom bombs dropped on Japan.

Tell them a story from the '50s. Who was the first one in your neighborhood to own a TV? Do you remember any of those crazy scenes from live television? Like when the saleslady couldn't get the refrigerator door open? Or when the newsman thought the sound was turned off? Or when the watch slipped off the elephant's foot? Describe what a variety show was like (since most of the current generation has never seen one).

And don't forget your views on the '60s, '70s, and '80s. Sure, there are plenty around to describe the most recent years, but tell your side of the story. Write about the traffic jam out on University Drive the day of the campus riots over the war. Or maybe you have a story to tell about when a Southeast Asian family bought the doughnut shop down at the mall. Tell them about your last trip to the Grand Canyon, and how it's changed so much over the past fifty years.

Even the events of today will be the good old days to another generation. Make a few predictions about what is going on and let them be the judge of your accuracy. What is the future of Communism in China . . . Russia . . . Eastern Europe? If you turn out right, they will shake their heads in awe. If you are wrong, they will slap their knees in glee. Either way, you reached through the years and touched them.

WRITE ABOUT THE JOYS AND SORROWS OF THE FAMILY

In your journal, make sure you write about the sorrows as well as the joys. Seek a balance. You don't want future readers to be depressed, but you want them to see things honestly as well.

You can tell them about how you and your mate bought that little grocery store on Broadway and 14th. You can tell them about how business boomed to the point that the store covered a whole city block. But don't forget to mention that wasn't the first store you owned. Tell them about the market down on State Street. You lost the house, the car, and your savings account when it folded— remember?

Excite them with stories of joy when Lucky Lindy landed in France. But tell them how you felt when you heard that Will Rogers and Wiley Post had gone down in Alaska. Tell them about how you scored the winning touchdown to defeat your dreaded rivals, and tell them how you struck out watching a slow curveball when your team lost the championship.

You don't have to dwell for pages on the topic, but tell them how you felt when the Marine sergeant showed up at the front door to tell you about young Bobby's death in Korea. Or when the doctor came into the waiting room and announced, "There's just nothing else we can do . . . " Or the day you sold the old home place and drove away from it for the last time.

Your life's measured by not only the successes but by how you handled the failures—and the sorrows, as well.

GIVE ANSWERS TO QUESTIONS ABOUT YOUR LIFE

If, for some reason you are still searching for something to fill up your journal, make sure you answer all the questions your grandchildren ought to be asking you but don't have sense enough yet. The day will come, we'd guess about ten years after you're gone, when they say, "Man, I wish I could have asked Granddad or Grandmother about . . . " So, do them a favor. Answer the questions ahead of time.

What will they want to ask? Probably all those same questions you should have asked your own grandparents but just never got around to asking.

These samples might touch off some ideas for you.

1. Give a room-by-room account of the earliest home you can remember. Describe the layout of the house—the furniture,

heating system, kitchen utensils, colors, textures, lot, garage, everything.

2. Describe grade school. Who was the best teacher you ever had? What made this one stand out? Who did you revere most when you were twelve?

3. When you were a teen, what different career did you want to pursue? Why?

4. When and why did you decide that Grandpa/Grandma was the one you ought to marry?

5. What was the smartest—and the dumbest—purchase you made before you were thirty?

6. If you had it to do over again, what one skill would you like to learn at an early age? Why?

7. If you could pick out one different era in history in which to live, what would it be? Why?

8. Describe, in detail, what attending church was like when you were a kid.

9. When you were first married, what did you pay for rent? For a car? For a loaf of bread? For a stamp? What was the pay scale for a good job? How much did you make?

10. Describe in detail all you know about your own grandparents. What did they look like? What was their personality? Occupation? Strengths? Weaknesses?

Perhaps these samples will touch off other ideas for your own journal.

Now we've got two last projects for you as you consider ways to keep the family history alive.

DESCRIBE THE PLACES IN WHICH YOU HAVE LIVED

First, hunt around and find a large map of the United States (or the world, if you need it). Make sure it is one that you can write on without destroying the leather-bound atlas or something like that.

Then mark down on the map the different locations where you and your mate have lived. Put a red X by the town, and the dates when you resided there.

Then, if you have the data, take a different-colored pen and do the same for your parents, your mate's parents, and your grandparents.

That way, at a glance, your family can see the geographical movement of your clan. Maybe the map will help your family see the clan's progression from Connecticut to New York state, to Illinois, to California, to Idaho more clearly. Your grandchildren will enjoy seeing the stability, or the mobility, of your family.

ORGANIZE THE FAMILY PHOTOGRAPHS

Second (and you just knew we were going to say this), go immediately to the closet where all of those old photographs are tossed in the Buster Brown® shoe box. Pull them out and identify them.

No, tomorrow won't do.

You've been saying that for years, and now you've forgotten half of their names.

Here are the rules.

- Don't worry about putting them in an album yet—that's the reason you've been so slow in doing it.
- Write on the back of the photos with a soft marker—one that won't fade, and one that you don't have to press hard and damage the photo.
- List the names of all the people you know, all the objects you can identify (like our old '39 Chevy coupe), and the year you think the photo was taken. If you have to guess, go ahead and do it. Just put a little *g* by the inscription. Remember, your guess is going to be a lot closer than your grandkids'.
- Then put your pictures in the safest place you can find.

Recently some neighbors of ours lost their house to a fire. Forty-six years of possessions were suddenly gone forever. There was only one thing they really grieved over.

"The photographs! We can never replace the pictures!"

They're right.

Protect them from floods, fires, earthquakes, tornadoes, and vandals. A fireproof file would be ideal, but that's not always practical or economical. At least, don't store them in the garage, or kitchen, or bathroom. Keep them high and dry and neatly boxed.

There's no reason just to tell your grandkids what life was like, when you can show them in pictures.

Your family history.

Grandkids who know their origins have an advantage over all the others. They know who they are, what they are, why they are, and where they're headed.

To fail to supply your grandchildren with their family heritage is to abandon them to an emotional and spiritual orphanage.

A journal, a map, a family tree, and a box of well-marked photos.

Not much of an inheritance to leave, you say?

Grandchildren who get all of that are the richest kids on earth.

6

Teaching Your Grandchildren Your Unique Skills

It's old, worn, and most often covered by a new silk bedspread. But every once in a while we peek under the covers and spot it.

Most folks would just see a faded, well-used quilt. The interwoven circles and stitching display the "wedding ring" pattern. But we see something different.

There's a screened-in front porch (not many of those left either). There are four homemade sawhorses and four long, narrow slats clamped at the corners. Stretched between the slats is a large quilt. The frame just about fills the whole porch. Over in one corner sits a gray haired, bent-framed, soft-spoken former Texas lady with a warm smile on her face and silver thimble on her finger. She will spend the better part of the summer stooped over that quilt until every stitch is in place. Then, when it is completed, she will fold it with love, and wrap it carefully in last year's Christmas paper she has ironed smooth for reuse. The only payment she will receive will be the smiles and hugs given in love on Christmas morning.

That will be enough.

You see, Grandma made quilts.

Not for money, though she could have used it.

Not for acclaim. The art critics would complain about her penchant for using up every single scrap of cloth in her house, no matter what the color or texture.

She made them because folks are supposed to stay warm at night. She had this notion that every man, woman, boy, and girl had the right to pull up a warm quilt over his tired, cold body. She couldn't provide such comfort for the whole world, but she could certainly take care of her family.

So she did.

Ah, they don't make quilts like that anymore.

There are a lot of things they don't make anymore.

The custom woodwork on the front of the houses has been replaced by molded plastic. Baking a cake from scratch now means merely that you didn't use the microwave. The lovely bouquet in the corner is made of imported silk flowers. The wooden duck was carved by a laser duplicator in Hong Kong.

The china cabinet in the corner is made of glued sawdust with stretched plastic photo of wood grain wrapped over the top and the entire piece stapled together by a robot. Behind the acetate-faced cabinet door sits an odd collection of dishes that are guaranteed to be oven proof, freezer safe, and nonbreakable.

Where have all the craftsmen gone?

Most of them died without leaving any protégés.

Your family, and the world, is just a little poorer because of it.

The trend can be reversed.

Maybe it will start with you. Teach your grandchildren some of those unique talents you have accumulated.

Why do we emphasize teaching grandchildren instead of children?

Well, your kids are all grown. It's too late for them. They are now submerged in that era where they are too busy and too intelligent to learn anything except how to make more money.

Now the grandkids, on the other hand—why, they're just about as foolish as Grandma and Grandpa and from time to time get bored because there's nothing to do. So we are suggesting a conspiracy between the oldest and youngest generations to keep the unique skills alive.

Know Your Talents

"OK, big deal," you respond. "I just don't have any skills to pass on." Well, if that's true, then get out there and learn a skill. What have you been waiting for? The truth is, you're probably loaded with talents to share, but you just don't recognize them. What we think is routine (because everyone in our generation could do it) proves to be unique in the current age.

For some of you, the first twenty years of your life you hitched a four-up team and sledded through the snow to feed the cows. There isn't more than one person in a 100,000 in our country today who could hitch up and drive four horses.

You called the pie riverbottom custard, because that is what your mother called it, and that is what your grandmother called it. It takes pecans, tart apples, white raisins, lemon rind, twelve eggs, sugar and molasses, a special mixture of delicate spices, twigs of clove, and about five hours to make it. Fifteen years ago you offered to teach your daughter how to make it, but she said, "Oh, Mother, you know I just don't have time for that. Besides, Barry likes the Pie Palace. I'd rather eat out."

So, like the California condor and circus parades, riverbottom custard pie is just about extinct.

For more than thirty years people stopped by your backyard on Memorial Day weekend and asked the same question. "Do you mind if I cut a few gladiolus to take out to the cemetery?" The answer was always a cheerful, "Help yourself." Flowers from that famous gladiolus patch of yours used to adorn half the tombstones at Rolling Hills. Your kids never had much patience to learn how to grow flowers. Besides, they had little motivation. They could always come over and enjoy yours. But now you and your husband are thinking about moving into that mobile home park. You know, the one that is mostly green outdoor carpeting and cement? Oh, it's a year or two away— just enough time to teach the grandchildren how to grow gladiolus— isn't it?

You might play an instrument, make cabinets, embroider pillowcases, paint landscapes, collect stamps, shoot a black powder rifle, write poetry, breed cocker spaniels, pan for gold, rebuild old cars, bake quiches, create Christmas tree ornaments, lay brick, or iron your sheets. Whatever your skill might be, it can be transmitted to another generation.

If you are having trouble finding your own skills, ask those around you, "What do I do well?" And, "What are my unique abilities?"

Start gathering your list. Add to it as you think of something else. This list is your target. Before you pass out of this world, you will want to make sure each of those skills is carried on by one of your family members.

KNOW YOUR GRANDKIDS

Even if they are still quite young, begin to recognize their particular skills and interests. There just might be one who exhibits real talent in a similar direction as yours.

Teach them all a little something of your abilities.

Our friend Curtis is an accomplished wilderness photographer. He might have made his living working for AT & T, but his love was obviously taking pictures. He has a standard procedure with his seven grandchildren. At age seven he gives each one of them an inexpensive 35mm camera.

It's a family tradition that Grandpa Curtis takes each child out by the lake on the seventh birthday and shows him/her how to take good pictures.

Then he takes the lesson one further. He promises to supply the film, and the developing costs, for any of the grandchildren who want to continue taking wilderness pictures. They just mail Grandpa the film, and he gets it developed and mails the prints back, with a new roll of film and a few suggestions on how each shot might be improved.

Out of the seven grandkids, only two or three have ever really continued to take pictures. But just last year, thirteen-year-old Carri began to send her Grandpa a roll every month. His smile sparkles as he talks of Carri. "She's got a photographer's eye, she does." He pulls out of his wallet a snapshot of a formation of Canadian geese flying only a few feet above the water. "And she's only thirteen! I'm getting her a wide angle lens and a developing set for her birthday. Why I wouldn't be surprised if she goes to work for *National Geographic* some day," he brags.

Curtis knows his grandkids.

And he just might have discovered the next generation of photographers.

Let them all experiment—but keep a watchful eye out for the one, or ones, who have unflagging interest and desire to learn from you.

KNOW YOUR BUSINESS

If you intend to teach a particular skill or talent, you will need to do a little more advance planning. Let's suppose you're going to give nine-year-old Ralphie a first lesson in woodworking.

You'll need to clean the shop. Put up some of the power tools you often leave within handy reach. You'll need to select the wood, lay out the pattern, purchase extra safety goggles, check on the carpenter's glue, purchase stain, put a new handle on that small hammer, pick up a small pair of rubber gloves, and purchase some more sandpaper.

Teaching a skill is not identical to merely doing it yourself.

Take time to consider the age and ability of the grandchild with whom you'll be working. Don't shy away from challenging him to learn new skills, but don't push him into a process that is too advanced, or too frightening, or too complicated for his skills. Set before him a project that, with a degree of hard work, he can complete.

Robert has spent most of his life in his garage. Most times the car is shoved out on the street because he's working on another project. There are shelves, cabinets, picture frames, flower boxes, coffee tables, and hope chests to be built.

In thirty-nine years of marriage he's collected about every tool imaginable, and some that few people on earth know how to use.

He certainly wouldn't think of turning the grandkids loose in his shop. But he doesn't bolt the door to the garage when they come over either. Robert's plan is like this: if the grandchild is under five, he gets to come out and sit on a stool and watch Grandpa work. This lasts about three to five minutes, he reports, but it gives them an idea of what he's doing. When they reach the six to ten age bracket he teaches them about sanding, painting, and pounding nails. In his scrap bin full of wood he always has a simple little project or two. When grandkids burst through the back door yelling, "Grandpa, do you have anything I can paint?" or "Can I help you pound nails?" Robert is prepared.

When they are in the eleven to fifteen age group he begins to teach them how to use the smaller hand tools, such as saws, planes, and chisels. It's also a time to learn about some of the power tools, like electric sanders, hand-drills, and jigsaws. At this age he lets them design their own projects.

At age sixteen and above, Robert figures those who are still interested can learn about the big power tools. He likes to encourage them to complete the entire project themselves, from wood selection to the last coat of varnish.

"Wow!" you say. "That sounds like the guy is teaching wood shop!"

He is.

"Do you need any help in the shop, Grandpa?" the kids shout as they meet him at the door.

It's a funny thing. For seventeen years now, Grandpa has always needed some help. It's almost as if he planned it that way.

Know Your Limitations

A five-year-old grandchild has a very limited attention span. You know that. And a seventy-five-year-old grandfather might have a limited teaching span. Understand that as well. Make sure the projects you work on together fit both your grandchild and you.

When you set out to teach a grandchild a skill, keep in mind the child's potential. If properly taught, what could this kid accomplish? Your goal should be to help him week by week, or month by month, or year by year to achieve that potential. The delight in teaching is not merely watching a talented student continue to excel—the real thrill is watching an underachieving, fearful student suddenly realize he really does have the ability to complete the project himself.

When Allisa was seven years old she spent a week with her grandmother at the lake. During that time, Grandma Martha spent the afternoons painting at the water's edge while Allisa played in the sand.

Each day the granddaughter carefully inspected her grandmother's work. By the end of the week, the painting was done.

"Grandma, that's the most beautiful painting I've ever seen in my whole life," Allisa sighed, "I wish I could paint like you."

"Well, I bet you could someday," Grandma Martha encouraged.

"Nah—not me. My teacher, Mrs. Melton, said my art wasn't good enough to hang up for open house."

"She what?"

"So now I just read a story during our drawing time."

That challenged our friend, Martha. Lord willing, and she lived long enough, she would work with Allisa until she could paint a lakeside landscape.

Of course, a squirmy seven year old had a long way to go. So Martha developed an ambitious plan. Each year, during their vacation time together, she would teach Allisa a different technique that would be necessary for the landscape. She didn't mention to Allisa where all the lessons were leading. In fact, Martha placed the lakeside landscape of hers in a closet out of sight.

The first few years were pretty basic—and humorous. Just little scratches of attempts to draw a tree or a rock. Every year's picture was placed in a "memory box." The occasional letters to Allisa would always contain a hint or two about how to draw better. On her twelfth birthday, Grandma Martha sent a set of oil paints. On her fourteenth, a beautiful wooden easel, and on her sixteenth a selection of canvasses and brushes.

In the summer she was seventeen, Allisa was once again at the lake. She had quit her summer job one week early to be with her grandmother the week before her college classes began. This time both ladies were down at the lakeside painting.

"Grandma, I've decided to minor in art. What do you think?"

"I think you'll do very well. You could come home and teach me a thing or two."

By Saturday, Allisa had almost finished her painting. "You know, Grandma, you probably don't remember this, but I used to hate art."

"Really?"

"Yeah, I didn't think I could do it. I was really embarrassed for anyone to see what I'd drawn. It seems easier now. What do you think, did I get that reflection of the sunset on the water bright enough?"

"Oh, it's beautiful," Grandmother Martha replied.

That evening Martha went to the closet and pulled out a dusty old painting that had leaned against the wall in the lakeside cabin closet for years.

"Do you remember this painting of mine?" she asked.

"No, not really."

"How does the sunset compare with yours?"

"Can I be honest? Well, I like mine better. I think I've captured how the light reflects, then gradually disappears into the waves."

"I agree. Allisa, I painted this picture about ten years ago. At the time you told me, 'Grandma, that's the most beautiful painting in the whole world. I'll never be able to paint like you.'"

"I said that?"

"Yes. And now look at you. You've just outpainted me."

"But yours is very nice, Grandma."

"Honey, I knew we could prove her wrong."

"Who, Grandma?"

"That teacher who said you couldn't draw."

"Yeah, I guess we did, didn't we?" Allisa hugged her grandmother.

Martha actually worked ten years with her granddaughter?

Certainly. A grandchild is worth a measly ten years, right?

Martha knew her own limitations. She could teach only a few basic concepts at a time. She was aware of how little time, per year, she would be allowed to work with Allisa. And she knew that her granddaughter could only accomplish so much at eight, nine, or ten.

But Martha looked beyond the jam-smeared freckles and the sand-filled, stringy brown hair and was able to see potential that others had missed.

Teachers are busy with a whole room crammed with students.

Parents are swamped by survival and necessities.

But grandmas and grandpas—the Lord has abundantly supplied them with the gift of encouragement and, sometimes, the gift of teaching.

Martha doesn't teach Allisa anything about art anymore. She doesn't need to. Her task has been completed. It was a job well done.

KNOW WHAT IT WILL COST YOU

Nobody ever said grandchildren were cheap.

Check out their Christmas list—how many presents do they want that cost less than $10? $20? $50? Shall we keep going? Being a good grandparent means investing more than money. It will take all your spare time and most of your patience to teach a skill to one of your grandchildren.

It means Sissy will cut the pattern wrong and waste yards of material.

It means Junior will burn up your new table saw.

It means Billy will hoe out all the carrots in your garden and leave only the weeds.

It means Christopher "borrowed" your 1903 stamp and used it to mail a postcard to Santa Claus.

It means your electric drill accidently got filled with woodworking glue.

It means you lost three cookie pans to the chocolate chip crematorium.

It means giving up a golf game every other Saturday.

It means having a little tagalong on your trip to Arizona.

It means having an all-day sucker permanently attached to the bottom cushion of your sofa.

It means finally learning about patience, repetition, and endurance.

It will cost you something to be the kind of grandparent who takes time to teach grandchildren.

But what in the world do you and I work so hard our whole life for, anyway? Just to have a little something extra for the kids and the grandkids, right?

KNOW WHAT THE SCRIPTURE TEACHES ABOUT GIFTS

There is a tendency in our day and age to have a limited view of serving the Lord. Excited by reading of the great events of the early church as recorded in the New Testament, we have come to believe that the only way to really please the Lord is by becoming a world evangelist, church planter, and theologian like a Paul, a John, or a Peter.

We divide up "spiritual gifts" into limited categories and spend a lifetime trying to figure out if the Lord gave us any of these. If our life, we assume, is involved with anything less than these gifts, it is —how should we say it?—carnal.

It's possible, therefore, to come to a chapter about how to teach your grandson to build a decent birdhouse and assume, "My, this isn't very spiritual!" But wait, there is another passage of Scripture worth considering.

In the book of Exodus, Moses has gathered the Hebrew people out of Egypt and marched them out into the wilderness. The Lord God Almighty has dispensed His laws to them on Mount Sinai, and now, for the first time in their history, they are to have a place of worship. The blueprints for the portable worship center, called a tabernacle, are revealed to Moses directly from the Lord.

But how will he get such a masterpiece built?

He will need some extremely skilled laborers.

Where does he turn? Listen to the text itself:

> Then Moses said to the sons of Israel, "See, the Lord has called by name Bezalel the son of Uri, the son of Hur, of the tribe of Judah. And he has filled him with the Spirit of God, in wisdom, in understanding and in knowledge and in all craftsmanship; to make designs for working in gold and in silver and in bronze, and in the cutting of stones for settings, and in the carving of wood, so as to perform in every inventive work. He also has put in his heart to teach, both he and Oholiab, the son of Ahisamach, of the tribe of Dan. He has filled them with skill to perform every work of an engraver and of a designer and of an embroiderer, in blue and in purple and in scarlet material, and in fine linen, and of a weaver, as performers of every work and makers of designs.
>
> "Now Bezalel and Oholiab, and every skillful person in whom the Lord has put skill and understanding to know how to perform all the work in the construction of the sanctuary, shall perform in accordance with all that the Lord has commanded." (Exodus 35:30–36:1)

Remember six key points from that passage:

- Bezalel has been called by name by God (v. 30).

The Lord didn't say to Moses, "Scout around for your best building contractor." He didn't say, "Moses, don't you have a guy with gray hair and bushy eyebrows who's a pretty good silversmith?"

God knew exactly what skill each one possessed.

Now Bezalel isn't known in history as a mighty warrior for the Lord. To our knowledge he didn't slay any giants, conquer any kingdoms, face any fiery furnaces, or utter prophetic words about end times. No Old Testament book is named after him, and his name is not chronicled among the heroes of the faith in Hebrews 11.

But the Lord God Almighty called him by name!

When the history of the great people of the twentieth century is completed, we might not be mentioned at all. But that does not mean God has not called us by name! You might never pastor a large church, lead an evangelistic rally, serve on the foreign mission field, cut a record, or write a book, but God calls you by name!

As far as the Lord is concerned, the work set before Bezalel was as important as any that needed to be accomplished.

- The Lord filled Bezalel with His Spirit (v. 31).

We live not only on this side of the cross from Bezalel but also on this side of Pentecost. Quoting the prophet Joel, Peter said on the Day of Pentecost that in our day God will "pour forth of [His] Spirit upon all mankind" (Acts 2:17). Therefore, we have grown up with the idea that every believer is allowed access to the Holy Spirit.

But what about the days before Pentecost? It is a rare thing to find a mention about a person's being filled with the Spirit of God. Certainly we can remember Moses, and Joshua, and David, and some others. But we can almost name them on our fingers.

That's why this reference is so startling. Here's a man, Bezalel, filled with the Spirit of God. What does he do with this wonderful relationship? He goes out and builds things.

If Bezalel took a modern survey to discover his spiritual gifts he might be surprised to find that "craftsmanship" was not on the list presented to him. It should be.

- Notice the specifics of the gift given him: wisdom and understanding and knowledge as they pertain to craftsmanship.

Such a passage elevates all skills and talents. Could it be that there is something God-given in the ability to lay brick, build fences, sew drapes, make goblets, and carve wood?

Yep. There just might be something spiritual in all of this.

Now one could protest that the spiritual nature of Bezalel's gifts had to do with the project at hand. He was called to create a tabernacle for God. Therefore, what was ordinary, common—even profane—now became spiritual, special, and sacred because of what was being constructed.

So, the theory would go, if you are using your skill for something dedicated to the Lord's service, then you are doing a spiritual work, and if it is for common use, it is nonspiritual.

There's a flaw in that argument, though. Jesus said in Matthew 25:40, "Truly I say to you, to the extent that you did it to one of these brothers of Mine, even the least of them, you did it to Me." So it's not merely what we do directly for the Lord that's included.

And Paul made it clear: "And whatever you do in word or deed, do all in the name of the Lord Jesus" (Colossians 3:17). That, in a blanket statement, sanctifies our every action.

Suddenly, every use of our God-given skill becomes something dedicated to God.

Tucked away in a remote attic of the nineteenth-century Shaker home we discovered a beautiful built-in closet. Handcrafted drawers and cabinet doors, even after one hundred years, displayed the perfection of the craftsman who built them. Why would anyone go to such meticulous detail on a cupboard that would never be seen? Because the Shakers hold to the view that everything you make should be dedicated to God and be pleasing to His eyes.

Bezalel had the spiritual gift of craftsmanship.

• Don't overlook that his gifts were described in specific terms.

He was a goldsmith, silversmith, and bronzesmith (Exodus 35:32).

He was a stonecutter (v. 33).

He was a woodcarver (v. 33).

He was an engraver (v. 35).

He was a designer (v. 35).

He was an embroiderer (v. 35).

He was a weaver (v. 35).

And just in case something was overlooked, he was skilled at performing in "every inventive work" (v. 33).

Now, how in the world did one man learn so many skills? There are those who would say that this Bezalel was just an ordinary fellow, but suddenly, on the day he came face-to-face with the Lord, all those skills were thrust upon him in a flash.

That could be. God is certainly powerful enough for such a task.

But we have a different idea. We think that Bezalel learned all the basics of these skills just like everyone else in his day—from his parents—and from his grandparents.

At the right time, and in the right place, God filled him with His Spirit and allowed him to supervise the building of the Tabernacle. But long before that some Hebrew grandmother had showed little Bezzie how to embroider, and some Hebrew grandpa had sat him down and taught him how to carve wood.

Perhaps the day will come in the life of your grandchildren and ours when God chooses to use the special skills we have taught them for a specific project such as this. Who knows for what future acts we are training them?

• The Lord put it in Bezalel's heart to "teach" (v. 34).

Bezalel's desire to see these skills learned by others did not merely stem from his own need to find disciples or fame. Don't you love this kind of a teacher? Every once in a while you run across a teacher who has a passion, a drive, a compulsion to see that others learn his knowledge and skills.

That's the kind of man that Bezalel was.

It would certainly take more than one man to build the Tabernacle. "No problem," we can hear Bezalel shout. "I'll teach them how to do it!"

Your strong desire to pass on your skills to your grandchildren might stem from a similar motivation. Perhaps the Lord has put it in your heart to teach.

• Bezalel isn't the only one so gifted by God. There were others in whom "the Lord [had] put skill and understanding to know how to perform all the work in the construction of the sanctuary" (36:1).

The beautiful Tabernacle was a result of many skills and talents. Hundreds of hours of hard work, relying on abilities they had learned from others, and the motivation of the Spirit of God were invested in its completion.

The kingdom of God will always need prophets and priests, teachers and evangelists, missionaries and pastors—and it will need weavers and carvers and those skilled at "every inventive work."

In biblical times, especially in the Old Testament, it was a sad event when a man or woman died and left no heirs. In some ways it is still sad to think that a certain name will die off because there are no future generations to carry it on.

Grandpa and Great-grandpa and Great-great-grandpa would be depressed to know that the lineage just stopped.

But perhaps we need a similar conviction about those special skills God has allowed us to learn over the course of our lives. They might be unique to you; they might be ones you learned from a parent or grandparent. Either way, your community and your family loses out when that ability is not passed down to a future generation.

Every skill and talent that is lost shifts civilization down to its lowest common denominator. You and I won't change a world trend by ourselves. But we can stop the decay in talent in one family.

Ours.

7

Support Your Grandchildren's Parents

We chatted with the couple at the table next to us as the restaurant's bay window seemed to magnify the setting sun on the Pacific Ocean. It was the end of the day, the end of the summer, and for the couple, the end of vacation.

"I miss the kids," the wife reported.

"We seldom get away by ourselves," the husband added. "But Lucy's folks came out from Texas and agreed to stay with the children so we'd have a relaxing five days."

"But I dread going back. Mom will have all the routines destroyed by now."

We probed for an explanation.

"Well," she said, "Richie will gripe because we don't buy him donuts everyday like Grandpa did. And Bonnie will insist she is old enough to stay up until ten because Grandma said she was. And Tina will whine when we don't let her pick out the videos to rent."

"Yeah," the husband responded, "and Derrick will probably have another of those black t-shirts with some hideous rock group on the front. 'I have to wear it,' he'll rationalize, 'Grandpa bought it for me.'"

"Sometimes," the wife moaned, "I don't know whether I'm happiest to see the folks come or to see them leave."

It's a dilemma that happens in more than one household. Moms and dads need to have the support of their children's grandparents in the tough task of parenting.

How can you spot a problem like this in your family? Look for these phrases . . .

- "Mother, I really wish you wouldn't . . . "
  Which means, "Watch out, lady, you're about to exceed the limits of hospitality."
- "Sorry kids, your *mother* won't let me do that. . . . "
  Which means, "Your mother is the bad guy, and I'm the good guy, but for the moment she has the upper hand and we can't do anything about it—yet."
- "Sure, honey, go ahead, but promise you won't tell your daddy I let you do it."
  Which means, "Daddy's rules are kind of flaky, and it is all right to disobey them providing you don't get caught."
- "Well, I certainly think we could relax the rules just this one time for Grandma, couldn't we?"
  Which means, "If you really loved me you'd allow me this simple pleasure with my grandchildren since there is no telling how few times I will get to see them in the future and besides the whole restriction is kind of dumb in the first place."
- "I'm sure your father must have *some* good reason for not letting you do that."
  Which means, "This is one of the dumbest things I've ever heard of, but they will probably get mad at me if I don't go along with it, so I'll play along but I don't have to like it and I might as well let them know how I feel."
- "Frankly, honey, it doesn't make any sense to me either, but this is your mother's house."
  Which means, "Grandchildren and grandparents know a lot more than parents about what is right and wrong, but we are held back because we don't have any real power in this home."
- "Well, my word, I don't know how my generation ever survived raising children without all the so-called experts around to tell us what to do."

Which means, "You don't have to read some book in order to know how to raise your kids. Common sense was good enough for my generation, and it ought to work for yours."

You've heard some of these before.
You've said some of these before.
At times you have disagreed on how the grandchildren are being raised.

SEVEN DANGEROUS AREAS WHERE YOU MIGHT DISAGREE

DISCIPLINE

Grandparents are not the supreme court to which an appeal of injustice may be made. They are the friendly professors of family life, who are always ready to give a little advice to young and old—if asked.

God created the mother and the father and then allowed them to give special oversight to a flock of small people called "the kids." They are to love them, provide for them, protect them, and, if need be, discipline them. The scriptural text states, "Children, be obedient to your parents in all things" (Colossians 3:20). Notice it does not say, "Children, if your grandparents don't agree with your parents, you may choose which to obey."

We all hope that we have taught our children well. We would like to think they grew up understanding God's rules for family life and are trying to enact them. We trust they have found a life partner with similar commitments and that together they have a family that honors and pleases the Lord. We hold onto the idea that they are wise enough to learn from your experiences and smart enough to avoid your mistakes.

We hope.

But even when they did not learn their lessons well—when they rebel against your counsel, even when they never seem to seek God's guidance—they are still *the* mother and *the* father, and thereby responsible before God for the discipline of the children.

If you have a disagreement over how to discipline the grandkids, here's what you can do.

- Publicly support your grandchildren's parents.

Eight-year-old Junior is staying at your house for a few days. On his first day he breaks one of the important rules: he does not pick up all his Lego blocks before his bath time. The punishment, passed down by his parents beforehand, is that he does not get to play with the Legos for two days.

"But, Grandma," he whines, "I'm only going to be here for four days, and I wanted to show you my giant big truck stop!"

You reply, "Oh, I'm sorry too. Well, let's plan on playing with those Legos on your fourth day here. You can show me the truck stop then."

"But you don't understand, Grandma. It's very hard to build. I don't think it's fair not getting to play with Legos just because I didn't pick them up."

Then you smile and say, "Sometimes we all need good rules to help us learn how to do things right. I think your parents have a pretty good rule."

"Well, this isn't very fun!" Junior pouts.

"Would you say making brownies is fun?" you add.

"The kind with the walnuts and the chocolate sauce?"

"Yep. Let's make some in the morning."

"Just you and me, Grandma?"

"Sure."

"All right!"

- Question discipline only when you can do it in private and only when you have reasons to support your concern.

Call your daughter up on the phone and ask, "Dear, I wanted to check something out with you. I wonder if it would be all right with you if I allowed Junior to leave his Legos scattered in the den for a couple of days. He has so many projects to show me, and it doesn't bother me a bit. I just didn't want to do it without checking with you first."

- Once you have appealed a disciplinary action, then let the matter be settled.

Don't bring it up again to your grandchildren.

Don't bring it up again to their parents.

Remember they are trying to set disciplinary standards they believe best for this particular child. They are working for lifetime goals, and they must live with the child everyday.

Some of your short-term measures might not fit the long run of their lives.

BEDTIME HOURS

How strange it is. We forced our own kids to go to bed by 7:30 but don't mind if the grandkids stay up until 10:00.

How *should* you respond?

Darling, blonde haired Trudy pleads, "Please, pretty please, Grandma, can't I just this once stay up until ten o'clock and watch this television show?"

You reply, "Oh, honey, I'm sorry, but your bedtime is eight thirty. I couldn't let you stay up later than that."

Trudy comes back with, "But Grandma, lots of girls my age stay up until ten. I don't know why my mother won't let me stay up later!"

To which you reply, "Well, Trudy, I've known your mother for years, and I can tell you she's a very good mother. And if she says eight thirty, then that's it. We'll do some fun things tomorrow."

"That's not fair," Trudy pouts. "You're always on her side."

"You're probably right. That's because Grandma loves you and worries about you almost as much as your mother does."

"Almost as much?" Trudy sniffles.

"Well, precious, the Lord only gave you one mother and one father, and I can tell you from experience, there is no one on this earth that can love you as much as they do."

(A thoroughly modern grandma would have one other advantage in this situation. She could say, "Trudy, I'll set the timer and video-tape that program so that you can watch it in the morning.")

FOOD AND NUTRITION

Your daughter-in-law insists that your grandchildren should not have any white sugar, white flour, white bread, or salt. But somehow you survived to a lively age not worrying about any of those things. So when the grandkids come over, what do you feed them?

Donuts.

Fruit Loops.

French fries.

Hot dogs on white buns.

And sugary red Kool-Aid.

That's just breakfast.

Or maybe it's the daughter-in-law that feeds them that way. It might be that you are the one that is health conscious. Either way, there can be a conflict.

The easiest way to deal with this problem is to major on feeding your grandkids moderate amounts of healthy food—few moms ever complained about that.

If you know some specific foods that her parents forbid, honor their wisdom. If you have a special reason to feed her something different, call your grandchild's parents ahead of time and ask permission.

"Honey, there's a new little bakery in the mall, and I wanted to know if it would be OK to take Violet there for some tea and sweets this afternoon."

You see, you have left Mom still in charge of nutrition. And you have proved that you are really not trying to circumvent that wisdom.

TELEVISION

At eleven every morning, every weekday of the year, you watch one hour of soap operas. So when Mercedes comes to stay you think nothing of flipping on the set. Besides, today is the day you'll find out if Sid is going to propose to Charlotte, or will he let her raise the baby alone? And if he proposes will Lydia have him arrested for breaking and entering? Not only that, Rodney is making a pass at Lydia and her sister, without the other's knowledge.

So when your daughter drops off Mercedes, she informs you, "Now, don't let her watch any of your horrible soap operas!"

This can go either way, of course.

Mercedes flips on some late night show about a lady dope dealer who gets raped and then goes on a rampage with a butcher knife. When you tell her to turn off the television, she replies, "But my folks always let me watch this program!"

The battle rages.

How do you settle the dilemma? Keep so busy with other activities that neither you nor the children have time to watch TV at all.

Radical?

Sure. But you can spend every other day of the year glued to the tube, and so can they. Don't waste any valuable time with your grandchild in front of a noisy, demanding box.

THE AMOUNT AND KINDS OF GIFTS

On Chad's fifth birthday, his Grandpa Clayton bought him a fancy set of cap pistols, complete with imitation leather holsters and fake plastic bullets in the belt.

On Chad's tenth birthday, his Grandpa Clayton provided him a deluxe Daisy B-B gun and a three-pound box of B-B's.

On Chad's fifteenth birthday, his Grandpa Clayton bought him a Remington 30.66 rifle, complete with scabbard, targets, and bullets.

What do these three events have in common? Each of these gifts made Chad's mother furious. She did not want her son having guns, knives, or bows and arrows. She would not even allow Chad to own toy soldiers, tanks, or jet bombers.

"Grandpa Clayton knows that I don't approve of those kinds of things!" she fumes.

"She's trying to make a sissy out of that boy," he thunders back.

As well meaning as Grandpa might be, he is not only creating a wedge between himself and his daughter-in-law, but also between Chad and his mother. He has set himself up as the "good guy" and Mom as the "bad guy." No present is worth that.

CONVERSATIONS HELD IN FRONT OF THE CHILDREN

A hideous rape and murder takes place in the same city where your daughter lives. When you stop by for a visit, she wants to talk about the crime. As she begins to give you the grisly details you notice your grandchildren playing over in the corner of the room.

"Eh, maybe we should talk about this some other time," you suggest, raising your eyebrows toward the children.

"Oh, they never pay attention to what we're talking about," your daughter replies and then launches into another description of the crime as you wince.

Your daughter, noticing your obvious discomfort, throws up her hands in disgust. "Mother, this has really bothered me. I don't know why you just can't hear me out!"

Conflict.

Should kids hear about murders and rapes?

Should the conversation in front of them turn to prostitution, homosexuality, adultery?

Should they hear about demons, ghosts, and Satan worship?

Should they enter into conversation about auto accidents, bloody bodies, and death?

Are there topics that are off limits for kids? If so, what are they?

Have you ever asked your grandchildren's parents what subjects they would rather you didn't talk about in front of the kids? Sounds like that would be a good place to start.

SPIRITUAL TEACHING AND GROWTH

It's a pain many Christian grandparents endure. Their very own grandchildren don't get spiritual teaching or training.

Your grandson, Mark, comes to spend a week with you during July. You say,

"Well, Mark, how's everything going with the youth group at church?"

"Oh, Grandma, I don't go to that anymore."

"What? How come?"

"Oh, it's too boring. My folks said I don't have to if I don't want to."

"And Sunday school?"

"Nah, I don't go there either. You see, Grandma, lots of Sundays there are dirt bike races, and I need to compete if I'm ever going to get really good."

You find yourself with a spiritually neglected grandson.

You will probably only have limited influence over what happens at his home. You can express your concerns to Mark's parents, but once they understand your position, then you'll have to back off. But you can set a different pattern in your own home. If you normally say grace before every meal, even when out in public, then don't stop because of the grandkids. If you read a Bible portion every morning during breakfast, then continue the practice no matter who's sitting at the table with you. If your habit is going to Sunday school and church, then insist that all who are in your home do the same.

When Mark, or his parents, complain about your discipline, just smile and say, "Oh, now, that's just the way I am. You know grandmas—they get set in their ways."

Why Grandparents and Their Children Differ About Raising Children

This last point brings up an important consideration. You must determine why it is you are having differences concerning how the grandchildren should be raised.

There seem to be four prime causes.

There might be a true biblical difference. Your grandchildren's parents could give your granddaughter permission to go on a two-week camping trip with her boyfriend. Just the two of them. One sleeping bag. For you, it's not just a social or cultural issue.

You can't condone the behavior, no matter how much you might want to support the girl's parents. When action violates the clear teaching of Scripture, you can never compromise. You can try to be sensitive to feelings, compassionate with your judgment, and loving with your reprimand, but you must take a biblical stand and accept the results.

But we said, "true" biblical difference, and "clear" teaching of Scripture. Some of our differences aren't as straightforward. For instance, you might be very determined that no decent Christian would ever attend a public movie. That has been your church's policy, and your personal decision, for years. It has worked well for you.

However, your granddaughter is allowed by her parents to attend some selected films at the movie theater. You might not think this is wise. And you might be right. But this is not a biblical issue. Caution and compromise are called for.

You might be having an environmental difference about how to raise the children. Your daughter-in-law opts for home schooling the grandchildren. But the whole process seems to you to rob the kids of a classroom experience with other children. As you drive to the market you pass the grade school in your town and see children playing all over the school yard. About half of the teachers in this school attend your church, and you personally know of their strong faith and commitment to children. You just can't imagine why your grandchild should be stuck in the house with his mother all day long. "All the rest of us survived public schools," you mumble to yourself.

But you don't live on the south side of the big city where any night you can expect to hear shots fired and sirens blare. You've never seen dope dealers hanging around the playgrounds of an elementary school. Your school district doesn't have openly homosexual teachers who flaunt their sexual preferences as an "alternative life-style" to their students.

The environments are different. And, just perhaps, the child-raising methods have to be adapted.

Your disagreements may center on different role models. A natural tendency is for all of us to think that everyone ought to raise their children exactly as we raised ours. Oh, we made a mistake or two, and we certainly don't want those repeated, but for the most part we did satisfactory.

We raised our boys on whole milk—there's no reason the grandkids should have to drink skim milk.

We ironed the kids' clothes every night before school. There's no reason why your grandchildren must wear wrinkled shirts.

We sent them off carrying a nice little blue lunch bucket. Our grandkids can do the same.

No decent girl ever had her ears pierced in our day, so there's no reason for your granddaughter to have hers done.

On and on the list goes . . . differences based on cultures, eras, fads, and preferences.

If we start any complaint with "In my day . . . " the battle has been lost. Let's face it—it's not our day anymore. Not our day to raise little ones.

Worry about your grandchildren if they aren't being loved. Pray for your grandchildren if they are not being spiritually taught. But relax a little if the differences are based on the changing tide of methods, styles, and theories.

If your grandchildren are well loved by their parents, if they live in a home where the Lord is honored and the Bible is obeyed, then everything else is just frosting on the cake.

Often the differences are due to personality conflicts and power struggles. These are the hardest to detect and the most difficult to admit.

Why does that classic friction arise between wife and mother-in-law? Because of a power struggle to control the life of the same man. To one he's her son, to the other her husband. And when the grandchildren come along, they are added as fuel to the battle. Whose will can prevail?

Grandma shows up at the house with a big box of chocolate candy for the kids. They are delighted. Their mother is irate.

"She knows I don't like them to eat that! But she does it every time!"

Now, actually, grandmother could bring them a big basket of fruit, and the kids would be happy. In fact, the mother could allow the children to eat a few pieces of candy from time to time without damaging their health or their teeth. But the war is not over health. It's over who controls this family.

Grandma defies, mother fumes, and the turf war heightens.

Unless the difference is clearly a biblical one and to compromise would be to disobey the Lord, then grandparents have no choice but to learn to support their grandchildren's parents.

No matter what kind of pattern you have established in the past, you can begin immediately to strengthen support of your children's parenting. Here are some places to start.

EIGHT THINGS YOU CAN DO IN ONE VISIT TO SUPPORT YOUR GRANDCHILDREN'S PARENTS

1. Walk in the front door of their house, and within three minutes find at least one thing about which you can sincerely compliment your grandchildren's mother within the hearing of the kids.

By doing this you establish the fact that your visit is not going to be a formal inspection.

2. Ask your daughter (or daughter-in-law) for her advice on a parenting problem one of your friends faces.

   If your best friend's daughter is struggling with how to cope with a strong-willed three-year-old, ask your daughter (or daughter-in-law) what she would suggest. By doing this you are admitting that you are not a parenting expert who has all the answers, and you immediately establish your daughter's (daughter-in-law's) credibility.

3. Before you visit, call your grandchildren's parents. Tell them you'd like to bring over a little present to the kids. Ask them if there is any particular thing they would suggest you purchase (or anything you shouldn't purchase).

   That way, there will be no surprises to explain. If they have a preference, you will please the parents as well as the child. If they tell you anything will do, then they have no basis for complaint. By doing so you have acknowledged that their decisions are of primary importance in the children's parenting.

4. Find a project that involves you and the grandkids directly and jump right into it.

   Sit down and read them a book, work on a puzzle together, play a game, review their baseball card collection, have a pretend tea party with their dolls. By doing so, you have given their mother a breather. She neither has to worry about entertaining you or watching out for the children.

5. If your visit is in conjunction with a special event (party, dinner, barbecue, graduation) go immediately to your son (or son-in-law) or daughter (or daughter-in-law) and volunteer your services for any job to help them out.

   Continue doing this even if they always say, "No, thanks, we've got everything under control." You signal the fact that this is their event and they are in charge. You willingly accept a subordinate position.

6. If it is polite to do so, defer any home leadership roles that are thrust upon you.

Your daughter says, "Well, Dad, I guess you always carve the Thanksgiving turkey," and hands you the knife. Just hand the knife on down to your son-in-law and say, so the kids can hear, "Oh, I'm sure Norbert can do it as well as I can."

7. Eliminate words and phrases with double meanings.

If little Lenora has a blouse with dried mustard stains on it, don't say in a loud voice for her mother to hear, "Oh, Lenora, I thought for a minute you had one of those new tie-dyed blouses! You know, honey, you would look cute no matter what old thing you wore."

You, of course, are not talking to Lenora. You are saying, "I noticed that the kid is wearing a dirty blouse. Don't you ever wash clothes?" The message is meant only for her mother.

8. Hug the whole family.

Not just the little kids.

Not just the children.

Demonstrate to the grandchildren that your love is the same for them and their parents. By doing so you show that you are not trying to build a special coalition that bypasses the middle generation. It's not you and the grandkids against the parents.

When your children were small, chances are you had an opportunity to sit in the crowd and watch them perform. You were there at your daughter's piano recitals when she froze up and didn't remember what to do next. You were there when your son struck out in the ninth inning of the big game.

You sat with pride and amazement that your very own girl was such an accomplished public speaker when she gave the commencement address, and you stood tall and proud as your son received the medal for courage from his commanding officer.

The point is, you knew they wouldn't always succeed, but you knew they wouldn't always fail either. Whichever happened you were ready to support, encourage, and console. Both you, and they, knew you were on their side.

Now your children are grown. And now that they are married, the family is expanded. But some things haven't changed. Your own children, and their mates, will continue to succeed and fail as they struggle with their own strengths and weaknesses.

Some of those failures will come in parenting.

But our position hasn't changed.

We're still on their side.

We're still there to encourage, support, and console.

We are not to demand a perfection from them that we in no way achieved ourselves.

Grandchildren are a resilient lot. Toss them into a cauldron of inexperienced parents, great love, personal struggles, forgiveness, spiritual sensitivity, a touch of pain and sorrow, lots of laughs, and supportive grandparents—and it's amazing how well they turn out, no matter what the parenting system.

8

If Your Grandkids' Parents Divorce

Christian grandparents raise Christian children who find Christian mates and produce Christian grandchildren. Then, the whole family lives happily ever after until the day the Lord returns.

A pretty picture.

We all hope it's true for our family.

We all pray it will be that way.

But it isn't always.

Christian grandparents sometimes raise children who never know the Lord.

Christian children sometimes marry unbelievers.

And, sadly, even Christian sons and daughters married to Christian mates sometimes never learn what it takes to make a marriage.

The result, so evident in our world today, is an epidemic of divorce.

We hope you don't need this chapter.

But lots of folks will.

Every person is accountable to God for his own sins. "Behold, all souls are Mine; the soul of the father as well as the soul of the son is Mine. The soul who sins will die" (Ezekiel 18:4).

Yet, there is a price children pay for their parents' sins.

Penny married Ted right after the war. Between 1946 and 1955 they had time to produce five children, fight the North Koreans and

Chinese, and fight each other. In 1955 Penny left the four boys and a girl with Ted one Friday night and never returned.

But since the marriage had been stormy, at best, they both said, "good riddance." After all, they had to do what was best for them.

Penny turned to singing in cheap bars and drinking cheaper whiskey until ten years and three husbands later she dried out and tried another attempt at marriage. She continues to struggle to hold it together as she raises a new family.

Ted fought to raise the kids in a two-room house in Salt Lake City. Live-in girlfriends came and went as the kids grew up with no notion of family stability.

All of the kids, the four boys and one girl, married immediately out of high school and moved out on their own. Ted then talked his best friend's wife into deserting her husband to marry him. This left the best friend's four teenage daughters in a single parent home. But, after all, the parents had to do what was right for them.

Of Ted and Penny's five children, there have been seven divorces and countless live-ins. Of Ted's stepdaughters, two have already divorced. They had to, of course, for their own good.

In forty-four years since their marriage, Ted and Penny have contributed, all or in part, to fourteen divorces. But the cycle hasn't ended. That's just as far as we can trace it.

Ted and Penny's is not a hypothetical story.

Nor a rare case.

It's just not that unusual anymore.

You could probably top this chronology with an account of someone near you. That's just the point. The sins and mistakes of one generation greatly affect the next.

You might not have been able to do anything to prevent your grandchildren's parents' divorce, but you can help minimize the damage it will bring in their lives.

And we do mean minimize—for there is no way they will escape unharmed. Parents who divorce are just flat admitting that they do not mind if their children go through life with an extra heavy load, a disability, a handicap.

But this chapter is not one dealing with the biblical view of divorce. Rather, it's for hurting families who deal with the fact of divorce, and the children caught in the wreck.

TEN IMPORTANT POINTS TO REMEMBER

- Most kids love both Mommy and Daddy no matter how rotten one of the parents might seem in your eyes.

The love of one's parents is a God-given affection. At times it defies logic and can even overcome a lack of reciprocal acts of love. Beth and her two girls took the bus to Denver to visit her sister. When they returned two days early she found that her husband, Kurt, had invited a college girl to live with him in Beth's brief absence. During the divorce proceedings she found out there had been many such "others." It has been almost ten years since the divorce was final, and Kurt has had a steady stream of girlfriends, lady friends, and a wife or two. His daughters, now in their teens, seldom see him. They never get a note at birthdays or Christmas.

They still miss their dad and often write him long letters that are returned, marked "no forwarding address." They love their father. No amount of outside discussion will change that. You see, love is not based merely on rational thought. Nor is it based on feeling. It is based on a decision of the will. They choose to show their father natural affection.

A grandparent does not need to set the kids straight about an errant parent. Instead, rejoice that the children still have a capacity to love, in spite of what they have gone through. Rejoice that the father (in the above case) is still genuinely loved by someone. That might be the only link he has to ever getting his life straightened out.

You don't have to lie about his character or his behavior. Don't tell the kids you think he's a wonderful father if he is acting like a jerk. But don't teach them that love is something that is earned only by good behavior. If God only loved us in that manner, who would ever be loved?

"But God demonstrates His own love toward us, in that while we were yet sinners, Christ died for us" (Romans 5:8).

- Your daughter-in-law may assume you are on the side of your child and, therefore, a potential enemy.

It's difficult to remain neutral in domestic fights. One of the tragedies of divorce is that it forces everyone to choose one side or the other.

One of our society's biggest lies is that divorce affects only two principal parties: the husband and the wife. At least two other groups suffer too—for years down the road—the children and the grandparents.

So, the divorce is final. The lines are drawn. Where do you fit? Most often on the side of your child. You've known him the longest, been responsible for his safety and happiness, listened more often to his tears and sorrows, and, no matter what will happen, will remain related to him for the rest of your life.

But some of the family is not on your side of the line anymore. Your former daughter-in-law, her parents, their friends, and maybe even your own grandchildren stand in the opposite corner.

You can't change this. Don't try. You are, and always will be, your child's parents. But you can try to soften the division. Most fights dwindle quickly when one side refuses to take a swing. Paul said, "If possible, so far as it depends on you, be at peace with all men" (Romans 12:18).

If facts are being twisted to wrongly accuse your child, you will need real sensitivity to speak the truth without sounding like a combatant.

Six months after their son Richard divorced, our friends Stanley and Margaret still felt estranged from Diedra and the girls. They weren't sure if they were still welcome. They felt awkward about visits because the girls always asked about their father. And they felt Diedra's apprehension about their motivation for the visit.

Their habit had always been to visit the grandkids every other week, and call them in between. But now they began to consider cutbacks. "Perhaps we should limit our visits to holidays," they considered.

Instead, they called Diedra and honestly confessed, "We want to be the very best grandparents we can for the girls. What would be most helpful to you?"

As it turned out, she wanted them to continue the familiar routine. "The girls don't need any other broken relationships." But now it was being done because Diedra requested it. She was recognized as the decision maker. Now she could welcome the girls' grandparents without being threatened.

- In most cases you will have no legal say concerning the children. Whether you are allowed to see your grandchildren depends upon the parent with custody.

One of the biggest fears of grandparents is that they will lose all contact with their grandchildren. The judge doesn't assure grandparents' visiting rights.

Gene and Norma Stites watched their dreams for Myles unravel before their eyes. Raised in a Christian home, young Myles rebelled against his parents, authority, school, and society. At age seventeen, his pregnant girlfriend and he decided to marry.

A few months after little Josiah was born, Myles was fired from his day labor job for drunkenness. The three came to live with Gene and Norma. Suddenly, Myles decided to join the Marines, and the three of them moved off to Georgia. Mom and Dad didn't hear very often from Myles and Kimberly for almost two years. Then Kim wrote a short note that she was expecting another baby.

Gene and Norma planned a trip to Georgia to see the new baby but were told by Kimberly not to come. Myles was in the brig and didn't want to see his parents.

Within six months, Sebastian was born, Myles was given a dishonorable discharge from the Marines (having to do with possession of drugs), and Kimberly filed for divorce. Both sides bitterly tried to prove the other an unfit parent.

Kimberly and the kids, and then Myles, moved back to the hometown after the divorce was final. The court ruled that Kim had custody, but Miles could have the children two weekends a month.

However, neither parent is particularly interested in the kids. They were just the prize of one last fight. Myles is so unstable he's seldom around to take his turn. But Kimberly allows Gene and Norma to pick up Josiah and Sebastian for those two weekends a month. In fact, she seems glad to get rid of them.

So Norma washes the children's filthy clothes and gives them much-needed baths. She's had to teach them how to brush their teeth, eat good food, and attend Sunday school.

Gene and Norma worry daily about their grandchildren's welfare. They would gladly allow the children to come and live with them. When they mentioned this to Kimberly she became incensed and would not allow them to see the boys at all for almost six months.

The grandparents moan, "Neither of the parents is responsible enough to have those little guys, but we can't do one thing about it. We just watch, and worry, and pray."

It's a fact of life too many grandparents have to face these days.

For now, their only role is to be an occasional island of calm in the tempestuous life of their grandsons.

- Both sides of the marriage will have their explanation of why the marriage failed, and you should make an effort to understand both sides.

After twenty years of listening to heartaches and headaches, after giving advice and interceding for hundreds of troubled couples, after watching dozens of marriages crumble all around us, we have come to realize that seldom, if ever, do we hear the entire story of how and why a marriage ended in divorce. People manage the information they release as tightly as a totalitarian dictator. You hear only what they choose, and most of the time they choose only what justifies their action and supports their side of the dispute.

No matter how conclusive the arguments and documentation presented from one side, you have got to hear the other side of the story. This is much more difficult to do than to say, especially for a grandparent.

Being forced to take a side, probably that of your own child, means you hear much about one half of the argument and little of the other. To your daughter-in-law or son-in-law you appear as an antagonist who won't really listen to them anyway.

It could be that you are alienated from your own child and take the in-laws' position, but then you have the same difficulty.

Beatrice was shocked when her daughter, Linda, called and said she had left David. She said she caught him having an affair with a woman at work. Since Beatrice had never heard any hint of anything wrong in the marriage, she was quick to take Linda's side.

But finally, after an awkward meeting at a supermarket, David sat down and explained his side. "Did you know," he said, "that she forced me to sleep on the sofa for the last two and a half years?"

Beatrice had not known. But now she knew. She knew that there was more to the story.

You have to talk to both sides. That probably means you'll need to initiate the conversation. Find a time and a location that is not threatening. Then ask the estranged one to meet with you and explain his—or her—side.

At this meeting you are going only as a listener. This is not the time to pass judgment. It is not the time to give your words of wisdom on how to straighten everything out. Just make sure you understand the situation from both sides.

Only then will you begin to comprehend the complexities that led to this tragedy. And then, perhaps, you'll be able to be a better parent—and grandparent as well.

- There is such a thing as a wronged party. Sometimes there is only one person to blame, and sometimes that one person is your child.

While you struggle to see the whole picture of the divorce you might discover that it was not a two-way street. Perhaps your daughter is right. It was all his fault. One person can break up a marriage no matter how hard the other tries to save it.

After twenty-three years of seemingly contented marriage your son informs his wife, "I need some time to myself." He divorces her and moves to Alaska.

That's it. No warnings. No complaints. No reasons. Just gone. She was wronged.

In Matthew 19:3-9 Jesus says that adultery is so hideous that it can actually rip apart the marriage bond. If one of them has committed adultery, the other is certainly wronged.

Sin is not justified by stating how miserable a person was before he committed it.

If one of the divorcing parties has obviously sinned, then repentance is due. All the love and concern you show them cannot overlook the sin.

- Unless the children are abandoned by both parents, your role is not to be a substitute mother or father but the very best grandparents possible.

You will not make a good mom or dad anyway. The reason is not in your skills but in the fact that in the children's mind they have a mother and father already, no matter how little they might see of them.

But this is a very freeing principle for you. You don't need to fill two roles (or three) but just the one—that of grandparent. The kids need to see through you that some marriages stick together, some relationships never change, some people can be counted on.

Grandma and Grandpa are supposed to keep right on acting like a grandma and grandpa. When your little Portia calls and says, "Grandma, I'm almost twelve. Don't you think I'm old enough to wear makeup?" you can say, "Oh my, honey, I haven't had to make a decision like that in years. That's something a girl and her mother ought to decide. But whatever you two come up with will be fine with me."

By doing this you have reinforced Mom's position in the family and yet shown support for your granddaughter. You don't need to make mother-like decisions, even though at times there will be subtle temptations to do so.

- Divorce does not prove that the mother was a poor mother, or the dad a poor dad.

Even the parent who might have singularly destroyed the marriage does not, necessarily, forfeit his parenting skills. He might have run away with the secretary, but he loves the children dearly, treats them well, spends time with each of them.

Most people in a divorce have a sense of failure already. (That is certainly true of the spouse who has been deserted.) They feel crushed as a partner and as a lover. If they have any sensitivity they will be depressed over the tough times they are putting the kids though as well. They really don't need any other failures.

It might sound like a simple thing, but when Woodrow and Estelle come over to stay the weekend you could exclaim, "My, how cute you two look!" Or, you could say, "My, those are the most darling outfits. Your mother certainly knows how to find just the right clothes for you, doesn't she?"

Just a slight difference. But Woodrow and Estelle's mom will hear it. You just implied, "Hang in there—you're doing a good job at mothering."

- Divorce does not necessarily invalidate other good qualities, skills, and achievements.

Divorce does not mean that they are incapable of doing good. If your son-in-law was a wonderful lawyer before the divorce, he probably still is. If you didn't hesitate to recommend him to your friends then, don't change your mind now.

If you viewed your child and his/her mate as perfect in every way, then, obviously, divorce will change your image. They are ordinary humans who succeed and fail, who can be righteous and wicked, who at times shine and at times fail miserably.

There's nothing about a divorce of which to be proud, but you can still enjoy your daughter's prominence at the university or your son-in-law's latest book. And you can be proud of those achievements in front of the grandchildren.

Gabrielle had always been a nurse at heart. She traveled the circuit of the family tending to the sick and infirm. She was the one who showed up with meals, ran to the pharmacy to fill a prescription, and did all the wash when anyone was down on his back. She'd sit up with you in the hospital and manage to be fresh and chipper the next morning.

Thirteen years ago she divorced the Anthonys' son and within weeks married a shoe store owner. They had seen her only occasionally since then. Last September, Lionel Anthony was in a serious car wreck. His wife, Andrea, stuck by his side for almost two weeks, day and night. The only break turned out to be Gabrielle's coming to spell her off at night.

When, finally, Lionel no longer lingered on the critical list, Andrea rejoiced to find that Gabrielle had cleaned the house and left the freezer stocked with casseroles. Whatever other faults Gabrielle had, and still has, her sense of showing help and mercy has not dimmed.

- Your model of marriage and family stability have become absolutely essential in the lives of the grandchildren.

When everything is going well in family life, your relationship with your mate is just one more building block in teaching the grandchildren what a stable relationship looks like. But when divorce hits a home, your example becomes extremely critical. It might be the only block left standing.

Therefore, because so much more is now riding on your example, you will have to work harder at a loving, open relationship with your mate. At times, you might even have to overemphasize certain aspects to help the grandchildren understand.

For instance, they might not see a wife and a husband forgive very often. Their parents, now divorced, seem never to forgive. And you two, being grandparents, always perfect, never need to forgive anything. At least that's how it seems in the eyes of a child.

There might be a time, although it could be awkward, where you let them know, "You know, I was so mad at your Grandfather when he went out and bought another fishing boat!"

With big eyes Cicely asks, "What did you do, Grandma?"

"Oh, I said a bunch of stupid things. Then I cried, and we hugged and made up."

"You did?"

"Sure. Some old boat isn't worth all that anger."

"Did he take the boat back?"

"No. Actually, I like the boat. It's a lot nicer than the other one. But he promised he'd never buy another boat without asking me again."

Normally, you might not even bother to tell young Cicely about that little scene. But she needs to see a couple that forgives. So you open up your life for inspection.

- Grandchildren whose parents are divorced will need more intense attention than your other grandchildren, but you cannot neglect the others.

This is one great reason why you can't be mother and father to your grandchildren who have divorced parents. You have others to whom you must remain Grandma and Grandpa. You don't need a stopwatch to clock the time you spend with individual grandchildren, assuring equal time for all. In different seasons, different ages, different circumstances, individual grandchildren need more attention than others.

But you can't make divorce seem like a reward.

"I always resented my cousin, Barbara," Denise told us. Her folks were divorced, so every Christmas Grandma gave her the biggest presents. 'She needs it more than you others,' I was told. It was Barbara who got to go on vacation with Grandma, Barbara who got Grandma's car when she turned sixteen, and Barbara who lived with Grandma when she got out of college.

"I can actually remember thinking, when I was about twelve, 'Boy, I wish my folks were divorced.'"

TOUGH SITUATIONS IN WHICH YOUR GUIDANCE IS ESPECIALLY NEEDED

There are at least three areas in which your grandchildren will be looking for your example.

FORGIVENESS

Often grandchildren become bitter at one, or both, of their parents. Usually this is caused because the parents refuse to forgive each other. Therefore the children have no model of what forgiveness looks like.

But forgiveness is a Christian imperative. We are not allowed by Scripture to withhold forgiveness. "For if you forgive men for their transgressions, your heavenly Father will also forgive you. But if you do not forgive men, then your Father will not forgive your transgressions" (Matthew 6:14-15).

Forgiveness is never simple, never easy, never fun. To release all forms of righteous indignation and truly accept a person who has crushed you and your side of the family is a gigantic act of obedience and holiness. To forgive often means to bear the brunt of pain.

But the kids and grandkids need to see your living example.

They must have a demonstration that forgiveness is possible before they chance it for themselves.

REMARRIAGE

Divorced parents have a way of compounding the crisis for their children by remarrying. This instantly doubles (at the minimum) the load of divorce misery that the children carry. All of a sudden they face father substitutes, mother substitutes, and stepsisters and brothers. They have new "grandparents" and new "aunts and uncles," none of whom they know very well and at whose home they always feel like an outsider looking in.

You, of course, don't necessarily want to share your grandchildren with another set of grandparents. Just as you have questions like, "Why in the world did she leave my son and marry this man?" so, too, the kids will have the same struggle.

Make it a high priority to get over such disappointments quickly. You have to be the one who keeps in view the long run of life when no one else seems to care.

You must ask yourself, *What kind of attitude do my grandchildren need in this situation to help them get beyond, to adjust for their entire life?* Obviously you do not want angry, bitter grandchildren possessed by hatred and self-pity. So you must demonstrate a kind of attitude and concern for the remarriage (or remarriages) that will wear well on the grandchildren for years to come.

When everyone else is leaping from day to day, you keep your eye on the long-term relationships and steer them in the right direction.

THE CHANNELS OF COMMUNICATION

Divorce can be so bitter and devastating that the one with custody of the grandchildren wants no part of his former spouse or of his family. Your former daughter-in-law might take the children and move to Maine. You have no idea when you will ever see them again.

What can you do?

Communicate. Write, phone, send tapes—whatever you are allowed. The children are the victims. Don't withhold your concern because of their mother or father.

Suggestions we gave in earlier chapters about long-distance grandparenting become absolutely critical now.

If you are told to stop communicating so often with your grandchildren, try to stay within the limits the parent suggests. But, for the children's sake, don't lose contact. Even letters that are never answered can express love.

If your situation is this drastic, make sure your correspondence does not bring up old wounds about the divorce. The situation is past. Now you want to be of help to the grandkids. Send them gifts, drop them a card when you are on vacation, call them on special occasions.

Second, pray. Surely you pray for all your grandchildren, but those who are taken away from your presence might need your prayer most of all. Pray for their safety, their maturity, their self-image, their relationships, and their salvation.

Divorce is a shipwreck.

Something went terribly wrong.

The dream of a united, peaceful landing is not going to be reached.

But it doesn't mean that the whole family drowns.

Grandma and Grandpa. Always there. Always the same. Always available for counsel. Always steady in their relationship.

They've rescued more than one struggling grandchild.

No one said being a grandparent was going to be easy.

Just rewarding.

9

Transmitting Spiritual Truth
to Squirmy Little Kids

Travis could hardly wait.

"I always do fun things at my grandma and grandpa's house!" he instructed his friends.

This visit was no exception. A couple of days later he reported to his neighborhood gang. "First, we went to Burger Den®, and I had a jumbo bacon cheeseburger. Then we stopped at the Ice Cream Palace®, and I had two scoops of double fudge. Next we went over to the toy store, and my grandpa bought me a triple pack of baseball cards. On our way back to their house we stopped by the video store and I got to pick out the movie. We watched 'Herman's Hungry Horse.' It was really fun!"

Travis had a good time.

But something was missing from the scene. Did you notice?

Travis eats at the Burger Den at least once a week. He always orders a jumbo bacon cheeseburger. There is an Ice Cream Palace about a block away from his house. He is one of their regular customers. Stuffed in shoe boxes at home are 1,800 baseball cards. And he has seen "Herman's Hungry Horse" at least a dozen times. In reality, the evening was just a repeat of his normal routines. We're happy that Travis and his grandparents had a good time, but it could have been better.

Nothing creative, nothing personal, and nothing "grandparentish."
We've heard all about the "songs and stories learned at your grandma's knee." But there is a real chance that such intergenerational teaching is becoming a thing of the past. You and I learned about everything from Mother Goose to Aesop's Fables . . . from Elizabeth Barrett Browning to Shakespeare . . . from Noah's ark to the three Hebrew children . . . from Uncle Remus to Lincoln's Gettysburg Address . . . right in Grandma's rocking chair. But where have all the teaching Grandmas and Grandpas gone?

"Kids don't want to sit still and listen anymore," we hear grandparents complain.

That's probably true, but kids don't like to brush their teeth either, yet every grandparent I know makes the kids brush. They need a teaching grandparent. Specifically, they need a teaching grandparent that reinforces spiritual truth. What is the grandparent's spiritual responsibility? Listen to Deuteronomy 4:9 (the italics have been added):

> Only give heed to yourself and keep your soul diligently, lest you forget the things which your eyes have seen, and lest they depart from your heart all the days of your life; but make them known to your sons *and your grandsons.*

And again to Deuteronomy 6:1-2:

> Now this is the commandment, the statutes and the judgments which the Lord your God has commanded me to teach you, that you might do them in the land where you are going over to possess it, so that you and your son *and your grandson* might fear the Lord your God, to keep all His statutes and His commandments, which I command you, all the days of your life, and that your days may be prolonged.

It's a strange but true fact that neither the Old Testament nor the New tells us that it is the responsibility of the church to be the primary teacher of the faith to the next generation. Passages like the two above make it clear that parents and grandparents are to be the prime channels of spiritual education.

The first verse above gives a warning to grandparents: *pay strict attention to your own spiritual life.*

You will have a tendency to forget the spiritual truth you have seen with your own eyes.

After you have forgotten them for a while, even the thrill you had in their discovery will fade from your heart.

So, continue to make mention of these things to your children and your children's children so that they will not be forgotten.

And then the second passage pleads: *obey the Word of God.*

By doing so you will encourage your sons and grandsons to do the same, and thus your family life will be preserved for generations to come.

CONVEYING SPIRITUAL VALUES TO YOUR GRANDKIDS

But how can you convey that spiritual truth to modern kids?

Don't . . .

- set up a pulpit in the living room and line up the grandkids in a row of chairs to hear your sermon.
- allow spiritual discussions to be relegated only to Sundays on the way to and from church.
- discuss theological arguments, church fights, and personality conflicts with the pastor until the grandchildren are physically and spiritually mature enough to handle these elements as adults.
- set God up in the sky with a big hammer ready to smash any child that disobeys.
- criticize other churches and denominations in front of them.
- put down the spiritual life (or lack of it) of their parents.
- make cultural distinctives (length of hair, skirts, and accepted activities) more important than biblical truth.
- make your love dependent upon their spiritual progress.
- expect to reach them with spiritual truth using the same methods that were effective for you when you were a child fifty years ago.
- unload all of your biblical knowledge on them during each visit.

What *can* you do?
You might try the following:

Whenever you talk of the "old days," make sure you talk about spiritual events as well.

"Grandpa, Grandpa! Were you here during the flood?"

"Noah's flood?" Grandpa laughs.

"No, no. The big flood of '49. We studied it in school last week."

"Yep, Bryant, I reckon I was."

"Well, what happened?"

"I remember it was on a Sunday that the river finally broke the banks. It had been raining for days. Late in April as I recall," Grandpa starts to explain. "Anyway, it was Sunday afternoon because we had just finished church and were scheduled to go down to the river for a baptism service. That was, before the storm hit. Most folks were disappointed to have the service canceled because it was the day Nicolas McCall was going to be baptized and no one wanted to miss that."

Wide eyed Bryant interrupts, "Who was Nicolas McCall?"

"Well, now, Nicolas McCall owned the newspaper in town for about a hundred years, or so it seemed. And most of those years he spent writing columns criticizing every minister, church, and Christian in town. One Sunday morning he showed up at the pastor's door at six in the morning, claiming he had to find out the truth about religion. Well, by the eleven o'clock service he had realized his miserable condition and humbly walked down the aisle and gave his heart to the Lord."

"Did he stop writing those bad things about Christians?"

"He sure did. And he invited everyone to his baptism the next week. But, as I said, the floods came, and we couldn't get near the river."

"Wow! Did he ever get baptized?"

"Oh, yes. You see, the water came washing down First Street right in front of the old church. There used to be a baseball field across the street in the lower end of the lot. Well the water stood about four feet at home plate, so the preacher, Dr. Filbert, just marched old man McCall right into the floodwaters and baptized him on the spot.

He said, 'Nicolas, the Lord has made it easy for you. He brought the river right to our front door!'"

"Wow, Grandpa, did the Lord really bring the river to the church?"

"Well, son, the Lord can do anything He wants. But one thing for sure, He used that flood to get Nicolas McCall baptized. That's how powerful God is. He can use everything in the world in order to accomplish His purpose."

Now Grandpa had a lot of stories he could have told about the flood. He could have mentioned the hogs floating down stream sitting in cast iron bathtubs. He could have talked about old man Johnson drowning while trying to save his horse. He could have mentioned how everyone in town went down to help carry goods out of the bakery shop but ate most of the donuts before they got them to the school for safekeeping.

But he didn't. He used this question as an opportunity to share a little spiritual history.

Openly demonstrate your holiness by proper behavior and by faithful devotions.

Grandma Housley's Bible is kept on the end table next to her recliner in the living room. It usually sits there next to the television remote control and the *TV Guide*.

But the *TV Guide* seldom gets opened. It's a gift subscription from a distant relative. The remote control has no batteries and has never been used—Grandma never could figure out how it worked. But the Bible? Oh, the golden gilding has long since worn off, the leather is cracked, the pages marked and bent, and cellophane tape holds much of it together.

It doesn't take six-year-old Allison long to discover which item is most important to her Grandma. When we ask her to tell us the difference between mommies and grandmas, she said, "Moms don't like to start the day without drinking some coffee first. Grandmas don't like to start the day without reading their Bible."

"My grandma gets on her knees to pray," Gregory reported to us.

"How do you know that?" we asked.

"'Cause, when I hear her praying in her room at night, I go to the door and peek," he reported. "Sometimes I hear her pray for me, and sometimes I'm so good she doesn't have to pray much at all."

Remember two things about the holiness you demonstrate in front of your grandkids:

- Make it sincere. Don't invent some phony behavior just when the grandkids come over.
- Make it consistent. Show your best holiness at all times. Whether they come to see you on a Sunday or a Tuesday, it should be the same. If you pray before meals at home, make sure you do the same when you take them out to the restaurant or eat a hamburger on the way home from the park. If they travel with you on vacation, demonstrate that you keep your same Bible reading schedule even there.

Make sure your grandkids have heard your personal testimony of how you came to the Lord. Eight-year-old Butch drew us a picture of his family. There was the typical house and tree, three big stick figures and four little ones, and a stick dog. Up in the right-hand corner above the clouds and the little birds that looked like the letter M, was one more stick figure.

"Who are the people in the picture?" we asked.

"That's my mom and my dad, my Grandma Jewel, my three sisters, and Buster, my dog."

"Well, how about up there in the clouds?" we prodded.

"That's my Grandpa Verne. He's in heaven, you know."

"Oh," we asked, "was he a Christian?"

"Yes," Butch smiled, "Grandpa told me that he was twelve years old and working one summer for a Christian neighbor who led him to the Lord after supper on the fourth of July."

"Wow!" we exclaimed. "You certainly know a lot about your grandfather. Did he tell you all that?"

"Yes, he did. We were very close," he announced.

We're sure they were. And somewhere up there, Grandpa Verne is smiling.

In sharing your testimony, tell them about what a difference Jesus made in your life. Maybe certain fears were taken away. Or certain habits conquered. Or relationships healed. Or direction in life given. Whichever, make sure they understand that life after accepting the Lord just isn't the same as life before.

Take them to Sunday school and church with you.

Although Marion had visited her grandchildren in Georgia often, this was their first trip to visit her in Seattle. She knew they would be with her for a week, and on Sunday they would all attend Sunday school and church.

So, the Sunday before they arrived, Marion visited the Sunday school rooms where the two granddaughters would attend. She chatted with their teachers, mentioned the girls would be coming, and took a good look at the classroom. As she was visiting, she noticed one of the younger ladies in her Bible study bring in her daughter. Marion chatted and set up a time on Friday afternoon for her granddaughters to get a chance to play with the friend's little girl.

During the week, Grandma Marion primed the pump, telling the girls all about what their classes looked like and what kinds of things they would do at Sunday school. By playing with the other little girl on Friday, she insured that they would know at least one other student in class.

When Sunday came the girls eagerly went to Sunday school, were delighted to have the teacher greet them by name, and felt instantly at home in the church.

Scenes like this don't just happen. It took one creative, hardworking grandmother. Fortunately for these two little Georgia girls, that is exactly what they had.

Spend time in a quality Christian bookstore surveying all the contemporary material available for their specific age group.

Don't rely on books you liked as a child. Don't rely on books you used with your own children. And don't stay limited to just books. The bookstore will have puzzles, games, videos, study booklets, picture books, and stacks full of creative material to teach spiritual truth.

Here are a few helps for buying good books for your grandchild:

- Find something for each child to call his own (even if the book is to be left at Grandma's).
- Don't guess at what age group a book is aimed for. Ask a clerk at the store. Most of them know exactly which books fit which ages, and if they don't they can look it up in the publisher's book catalog.
- If it is at all possible, buy quality printed and illustrated books. Cheap books don't last. Think of it as an investment, a legacy to be passed down to another generation.
- Look for stories that will last. Try to find books that will relate for years to come.
- Make sure the spiritual message of the book comes across clearly and that it is scriptural. If you can't easily figure out the message of a book, chances are neither can your grandchild.
- Examine the illustrations. Do they really reflect the message? Do they present a realistic presentation? (Does the text of the Bible say that Jesus floated mystically above the ground every time He moved about while here on earth? Then don't buy pictures of Him doing it that way.) Do the pictures inspire or scare?
- Ask the clerk about the author. Is the publishing house a reputable one? Every once in a while an off-the-wall slips into a bookshelf.
- If it fits in your schedule, take the grandchildren with you to the Christian bookstore. It will save you a lot of time if you have visited the store previously and selected two or three options from which to choose.

If you haven't browsed through the children's section at a Christian bookstore recently, you might be surprised at the creative, helpful, and inspiring material available.

Use the holidays to reinforce spiritual truth.

Christmas, Easter, and Thanksgiving are obvious times to remind all of the grandchildren of their real meanings. Your Thanksgiving card should have something more than smiling turkeys. Christmas cards must mention the birth of Jesus. Easter cards need more than pastel bunnies and eggs.

But sending a "religious" card, or even a tract, is not enough. Kids seldom read all the print on them anyway. So, in addition to those spiritual cards, write a note in the card personally mentioning your feelings for the Lord during the holidays.

- "Collin, I was just thanking the Lord the other day for what a wonderful grandson I have. You are one of the people He uses to make my life so special. Thanks for being you. Love, Grandpa."
- "Juliet, I just love Christmas, don't you? Especially the songs, and the decorated tree, and the presents. And to think the greatest present of all was when God sent His only Son Jesus to be our Savior. It's His birthday, and we get all the presents! Wow, we have a great God, don't we! Love, Grandma."
- "Wesley, isn't Easter a fun time? On Good Friday we are all sad remembering that Jesus had to die for us. But on *Easter* Jesus rose from the dead! It just goes to show how powerful and loving our God is. It always makes me feel as fresh and pretty as those new spring flowers. Love, Grandma."
- "I can't believe it—Clarissa is ten years old! I'm sure glad the Lord allowed me to be your Granddad. Have a great birthday, and remember I'm going to keep right on praying for you no matter how big you get. Love, Granddad."

If your grandchildren spend the holidays with you, you can do even more. You could have some appropriate Scriptures to read, prayers to offer, and times to reflect on God's goodness and provisions over the years.

Give some presents with a spiritual purpose, but include fun gifts as well.

Don't get the reputation "Grandma never gives me anything fun!" So buy the best children's study Bible on the market, *and* a top quality Little League baseball bat. Give them a cassette tape of delightful Christian tunes for children, *and* that adorable teddy bear you saw at the department store.

Demonstrate that you care about all areas of her life.

One grandmother reported that she uses gift giving as a special time of correspondence with the grandkids. In each letter she talks about the true meaning of the holiday. But she also includes a toy catalog. Then she writes, "Honey, I've marked some toys that Grandma wants to buy you, but I just can't make up my mind. How about you picking your favorite five from the ones I marked in red?"

Her grandkids spend literally days making and remaking their list from Grandma's catalog. Then they have to write back to her with the results. The kids learn two clear facts about Grandma: she always talks about the Lord, and she really likes having fun.

Read, read, read to them.

We have never, in any part of the country, ever found a child who was read to too often.

Never.

Ever.

Read to them Bible stories, missionary stories, Christian adventures, lessons from science and nature, biographies of famous Christians in the past, magazine stories, and poetry. Every opportunity you have to sit them down in the chair beside you and read . . . do it.

Shared stories provide a real bonding. We believe it is a much deeper experience than sharing a television program or even a Christian video. Movies and videos and television have captured, for all time and for everyone to see, particular scenes and dialogues. It is never new because someone has seen it before you. And because others will see it after you, it does not in any way belong to you personally.

But a book is different. No matter how many times others have or will read it, when you and your grandchild walk into C. S. Lewis's land of Narnia for the first time, it is a brand new, never before happened adventure. And what you experience together, and what you depict in your minds, will be uniquely yours to remember.

Few things in your schedule (certainly not doing the dishes, watching the news on television, or taking the dog for a walk) are more important than responding with agreement and delight to the plea "Grandma? Would you read me a story?"

Always give your grandchildren complete Bible answers to their spiritual questions.

If the concepts are too hard for them to understand, give them the concepts anyway. You are planting truth in their minds, and maybe the day will come when it all makes sense to them.

When five-year-old Sheldon dashes in and exclaims, "My friend Fudgwith says everybody is going to go to heaven. Is that right, Grandpa?" You will have to say, "No, Sheldon. The Bible says there are two places where people could end up. One is called heaven, and the other is sometimes called the lake of fire." Then turn to an appropriate scripture in your Bible (such as Revelation 20:13-15 and Revelation 21:1-4) and read it to him.

Now, you say, "A five-year-old kid can't grasp all of that." You're right. But a five-year-old kid has a terrific memory, and you have filed genuine spiritual truth into the mind that will be available at another time.

When six-year-old Rachael grabs your arm and says, "Grandma, does the Bible tell us who we should marry?" You can say, "No, but it tells us who we can't marry. We can't marry someone who does not love and believe in Jesus. Then read to her a verse like 2 Corinthians 6:14, "Do not be bound together with unbelievers . . . "

But, you say, she's only six.

True, but you can't guarantee you'll be around when she's twenty and ready for marriage. And even if you're around, she might not seek your counsel. But you have sensitized her conscience to the truth of God's Word and set a foundation for a concept she will have to deal with at some time.

Grandchildren Who Seem to Be Totally Unresponsive to the Gospel

Now, how about those grandchildren, some young and some old, who are completely unresponsive to the gospel? In fact, they are hostile to any form of Christian witness at all. How should you treat them?

Exactly the same as all the others.

The points above fit them just as well.

Your striving to share your faith is a statement about yourself. You are reinforcing to them that this is something real to you, something crucial in your life, something that for you is real, alive, and valid.

Don't back away from it for a moment. But don't expect quick results either.

When Renée was seven years old her grandmother gave her a Bible. It didn't happen to be a children's Bible with easy words or pleasant pictures. It was just an inexpensive King James Version Bible. Renée looked at it a time or two and stuck it in the back of a dresser drawer. After that her grandmother often gave her Christian books and objects for presents. But Renée threw those away. She didn't want any of her friends thinking she was "religious."

But she didn't toss the Bible, mainly out of superstition. It seemed like an unlucky thing to do. At age eighteen Renée married. As she packed her belongings, her sister reached in the dresser and tossed her the Bible.

"Here, this must be yours. It has your name on it." Renée placed the Bible in a cardboard file box that contained high school annuals and other memorabilia from childhood. At her new home, that box was shelved out in the garage.

Since Renée's husband, Owen, was not a Christian, they found no need to have a Bible in the house, and it remained in that box through seven moves and two childbirths.

One day, in a period of depression about the complexities of life and the helplessness she felt in trying to raise children, the thought occurred to Renée that some people found help in the Bible. Certainly her grandmother had.

Almost embarrassed to mention it to her husband, she finally squeaked out, "Owen, why don't we start reading the Bible?" To her surprise he said, "Sure." Then he added, "Do we have one?"

They rummaged through the garage and found the dusty black book with the cracking simulated leather cover. Night after night they read to each other after the children were in bed. The more they read the more they realized their separation from God.

Finally, after several months of this they began to attend a church in town. A few weeks later at a home Bible study they learned how a person becomes a Christian, and later that month both Renée and Owen accepted the Lord.

Now, twenty years later, they serve in full time Christian ministry.

It took seventeen years for the present from Grandma ever to be read. But Renée and her husband's conversion was no accident. It took a grandma who did what was right, no matter what the initial response.

We cannot force our children, or our grandchildren, to become Christians. But we can make sure every one of them has an opportunity to hear the gospel.

It's our privilege.

And our duty.

10

Teaching Proper Behavior
Without Nagging

Saturdays are lousy days to go to an amusement park.

Everybody and his grandmother packs in a few acres of expensive rides and stale popcorn.

But, sometimes Saturday is all you have.

So we stood in line with Aaron waiting for thirty-five minutes for some gadget to whirl us unmercifully through space until we all had stomach cramps. As we did, we watched one lady with youngster in tow.

"Gwendolyn, you are going to sit!" she barked as she flopped down on a bench and sighed deeply.

"Grandma! Grandma! Come on, we haven't finished!" The young lady pranced from one foot to another.

"Sit down!" The grandmother spoke with such a forceful tone that most of the small children standing in line around us started to sit.

"Oh, Grandma—this isn't any fun!" Gwendolyn pouted.

"Fun? Fun!" Grandma wailed, "You spilled Coke all over my dress on the train ride. You got scared at the top of Mystery Mountain and we had to walk back down. You ordered the most expensive dinner in the sky restaurant and then wouldn't eat it. You cried for a glass dinosaur and then broke it. You've had me standing in lines for almost six hours, and I have somehow lost an earring that's now been trampled by six million pushing, shoving kids. How much more fun do you think Grandma can take? Young lady, sit down!"

Gwendolyn sat down for about thirty seconds, then jumped up and ran for the line at something called the Suicide Chute. Grandma struggled from the bench and disappeared into the crowd.

We're sure they will both look back on this memorable day. But we're just not sure they will both think of it as a good memory.

How do you get grandchildren to mind?

Oh, sure, your grandkids are perfect. How about others, who are less fortunate? How do they get their grandchildren to mind?

Getting Grandchildren to Mind

Accept the fact that you do not have the prime responsibility for teaching them proper behavior.

That role belongs to their parents. You will certainly have a role in helping them learn discipline, but you don't carry the whole burden.

Let's say your fourteen-year-old granddaughter, Kristian, is having trouble with her classes in school. Her eating habits aren't too good, which results in a poor complexion. In addition, neither you nor her mother think she dresses very well.

On Friday night, Kristian comes to stay with you for the weekend. You haven't seen her in a few weeks and look forward to the time together. She bounces into your house, pecks you on the cheek, grabs a Coke out of the refrigerator, and heads for your den and the telephone.

OK, what are the goals for the weekend?

Well, you'll give her a lecture on studying, pump six healthy meals into her body, buy her some decent clothes, and teach her the fine art of reading a classic book instead of talking on the phone.

Wait!

It can't be done.

No kid on earth can change that much, that fast. So, relax.

Make up your mind where you can help and leave the others alone —for now.

Let's say you want her to learn to experience some of the better quality arts, to help her to move beyond television and telephones.

So you get tickets for the two of you to view a foreign folk dance troupe on Saturday night. You know for a fact that they are extremely good.

But you know it will take quite a feat to talk her into going. So this will help. Take her out for pizza (or whatever she chooses) beforehand. Let her wear anything of hers that is moral. And when you get home after the performance, let her call a friend and tell her all about it.

You can't change everything at once, and you can change very little in one weekend.

But that's all right because you aren't responsible for everything about her.

Discipline will be easier when you accept your limitations.

Always expect the best from them.

Let them know that Grandma and Grandpa are counting on their best behavior. Be realistic, but view them always from the highest potential.

Xavier is only six and has a tendency to never sit still. You've just bought him a nice, pretty yellow shirt. He loves it so much he wants to wear it to the Chinese restaurant for dinner. Your first thought is, "No way! He'll squirm around and spill food."

Yet, that's merely expecting the worst. It might be better to say, "Sure, Xavier. That shirt really looks nice on you. But, listen, you will need to sit still during dinner so nothing gets spilled on it. I'm sure you can do that, right?"

Some behavior problems are serious because no one ever expected anything better of the child.

"You always find a way to get into trouble!" we say, and the kid tries to live up to his reputation.

By expecting the best you . . .

- are quick to forgive and allow them to try again
- help them see beyond their present self-image
- give them an idea beyond peer standards for which to aim.

But—they have to know what you are expecting.

Don't require your grandson to rise to his feet when a lady enters the room if no one has ever taught him to do so. Nor should you presume that your granddaughter will sit perfectly still during an hour's church service if she can't land in one place for ten minutes at home. So, if need be, teach what behavior is acceptable in different circumstances. Just remember . . .

- teach only one lesson at a time. Don't try too many changes at once.
- teach when there are no immediate problems. (For instance, explain good manners when you are at home, not when you are at your neighbor's formal party.)
- teach behavior patterns that will truly be helpful for them, not merely ones that are helpful for you. You want Zachariah to get off his knees on the stadium cushion so he doesn't drop any more peanuts. The only problem is, when Zachariah sits down he cannot see any of the game. What he needs, rather, is a way that he can be obedient to you *and* see the event in the stadium. Keep his best interest in mind.

Don't force them to act beyond their age.

An eight year old is not expected to act like a twenty-five year old, but compliment them if they do.

Kids have an amazing ability to act their age. The trouble is we forget how a kid their age is supposed to perform.

Kids under ten pick out a place to eat because of the free toy premiums or the playground equipment. It has nothing to do with food.

Boys twelve to eighteen pick out a place to eat that offers the most food possible. Volume is the main ingredient—quality matters little.

Girls between twelve and fifteen will want a restaurant that offers views of and conversations with the cutest boys.

Girls between sixteen and eighteen will want very little food, and will probably select a place where no one will see them eating with their grandparents.

So don't let any of this surprise you. They are only acting their age.

Five-year-olds will love to go fishing with Grandpa. In fact, they will cry to get to go. But that will last about six minutes. Then they'll want to come home. Twelve-year-olds will fish with you all day long and half the night without tiring. Sixteen-year-olds know all there is about fishing and would rather you did not tag along after them. And twenty-five-year-olds will really enjoy fishing with you again.

You can force an eleven-year-old boy to wear a black bow tie to the piano concert, but please don't expect him to like it. Most fellas we know are about fifty-five before they like wearing a bow tie.

Nine-year-old boys shout.

Twelve-year-old girls giggle.

And six-year-olds will sing and dance on top of the kitchen table to get a little attention.

Teach them to be considerate.

Teach them manners.

Teach them to be careful.

But don't punish them because they don't act like grownups.

If the Lord wanted everyone to act mature He would have skipped the childhood stage of human development and let us all start as adults. The only thing really predictable about grandkids is that they will act exactly their age.

Personally demonstrate what you expect from them.

You must be a living example and model of the behavior you strive for them to achieve.

You hope that little Quincy will not embarrass you when the Garden Club comes over, but he uses a string of four letter words he learned from listening to Grandpa on the golf course.

You mumble at Evangeline not to talk with her mouth full, but she barely hears you because of the juicy tidbit you needed to share with your friend down the street.

You want Vergil to be considerate and helpful as he rides his bike on the sidewalk with other kids in your neighborhood, but instead he acts just like Grandpa does on the freeway.

Paul once made a very bold statement. "Be imitators of me, just as I also am of Christ" (1 Corinthians 11:1).

Remain calm. Refuse to raise your voice. Practice consistent kindness. If you exemplify the best of behavior, they will always have a clear target for which to aim.

Three key areas to look at:

- *prejudice*—a negative prejudgment of another person solely based on such external factors as a difference in race, social status, financial condition, or outward appearance (clothes, hair, make-up, and so on)
- *gossip*—telling stories (true or untrue) about other people for your own personal motivation and profit
- *self-centeredness*—trying to arrange everything in life to bring personal peace and comfort to you no matter what it causes in others' lives

Children often imitate the people they love the most. Every open flaw in your behavior will have little eyes watching. They are waiting for an opportunity to act just like their grandparents.

Show consistent concern about more than just the present moment's problem.

Kids have it rough. For the first three years of their life everyone wants them to walk and talk. Every visit to Grandma's centers on how many steps are taken and how many times they say "Nana" or some equivalent.

Then, just when he's getting good at running around and talking, everybody tells the kid to sit down and be quiet.

In the midst of this confusion, grandparents have the freedom to focus on long-range goals.

Short-range goals include things like . . .

- talking her out of wearing that bright red lipstick
- lecturing him about how horrible it is to get a *D* in English
- not letting him go "Yuuck!" when his aunt kisses him
- making him eat lima beans before he gets any pie
- teaching her not to climb trees while wearing her Sunday dress
- making him eat all the crust of his peanut butter and jelly sandwich
- teaching her not to leave her rubber duck floating in the toilet
- forbidding him to listen to rock music on your expensive home stereo system

We don't have to ignore these things. Rather, make sure our grandchildren know that these things aren't nearly as important to us as long-range goals.

Long-range goals include things like . . .

- knowing Jesus Christ as personal Lord and Savior
- learning how to unselfishly love other people
- finding a lifetime occupation that brings joy, comfort, and help to other people
- marrying a Christ-centered mate who will be able to bring out their very best
- taking a responsible role in their community with the highest moral and ethical standards
- helping them build a stable home environment in which to raise your great-grandchildren
- making their gifts, talents, and ministries available to Christ's Body, the church

Your list will go on and on. But notice the different types and significance of the items on the two lists. We've got to help them understand the difference between the urgent, present moment . . . and the everlasting.

Once you make your priorities clear in this area you might be surprised how it helps ordinary discipline. First, when it finally sinks into a grandkid how deeply his grandparents are committed to him, he will actually try to please more on the ordinary matters. Second, you'll find yourself letting up on some peripheral items of concern and therefore have fewer conflicts.

Explain to them not only what you want them to do, but why you want them to do it.

Perhaps Mom and Dad only have time to say, "Because I say so, that's why!" But Grandpa and Grandma should have enough time for some explanations.

"Grandpa, why do we have to say a prayer before we eat?"

"Because it's a constant reminder that the Lord provides all our daily needs."

"Grandma, why can't I rent an R-rated video?"

"Because those movies can mess up your mind. They can put things into your mind that you can never take out."

"Grandma, what kind of scenes do they have?"

"Well, some of them show bloody scenes about people getting murdered. And some have sex scenes showing things that God says are too private for others to watch."

"Grandpa, why do I need to shake hands with your friends?"

"Well, son, it's a friendly way to tell a person that you are happy to get to know them. To refuse to shake hands is like refusing to kiss your mother good night."

"Grandma, why do I have to drink milk?"

"Because it's filled with calcium and you've got growing bones that are made up of lots of calcium. Grandmas need calcium, too."

"Grandpa, why can't I run around the swimming pool?"

"Because all that water on the sidewalk makes it very slick and easy to slip. Then the cement is very hard, so if you were to slip, it could really hurt. I just don't like hurting myself, do you?"

Even if you aren't sure they understand the explanation, or even if they don't accept your logic, explain why it is you want them to behave. They will at least know that it isn't an arbitrary decision but one based on what you consider to be good reasons.

Whenever possible, teach the biblical basis for your behavior.

Let them see how you are trying to be obedient to the Bible. But remember these guidelines.

- Demonstrate your own obedience first, before you require it of them.

Sterling came over to your house just as you were on the phone with the chairman of the Women's Auxiliary. The chairman decided to cancel your talk again this month. "Well, I'm certainly not going to the meeting tomorrow!" you announce.

Later, Sterling comes running in with a complaint. "Percival won't share his cars! I'm not going to his birthday party!"

"Oh, no, Sterling," you explain, "the Bible says we should forgive each other, just as the Lord forgave us" (Colossians 3:13).

Great verse. Great lesson. Only demonstrate it before you make Sterling obey it.

- Don't strain interpretations just to get them to behave.

Melissa asks, "Grandpa, why did Mr. Neillor die?"

Grandpa answers, "Oh, because he drank too much whiskey, and you know what the Bible says, 'The wages of sin is death'" (Romans 6:23).

That's a great verse. Central to our faith. But is that the correct interpretation? Isn't Paul speaking about a spiritual death and separation from God? Melissa may think that if she, or anyone, ever sins, she will immediately die physically. And that's not a biblical view.

- Don't use "God will be mad at you if you misbehave" as a threat.

"Roscoe, you quit throwing rocks at that cat, or the Lord will get you."

Roscoe might even stop with the rocks—for a while. But the chances are, if he starts it up again, there will not be lightning from heaven nor will the earth open up and swallow him. So sooner or later, Roscoe figures that God doesn't care what he does or that you don't know what you are talking about—or both. Don't ever set God up as the mean judge in the sky. Far too many people in our country have wrong views of what God is like, and we don't want to add to that number.

- Allow them to point out any Scripture that might show a weakness in your behavior.

You just gave young Nathan a stern lecture on how the body is the temple of God. As a proof text you quoted from memory 1 Corinthians 6:19-20, "Or do you not know that your body is a temple of the Holy Spirit who is in you, whom you have from God, and that you are not your own? For you have been bought with a price: therefore glorify God in your body."

Having completed your discourse on the evils of taking drugs that change the chemical makeup of your body, you pull out your favorite pipe, stuff it full of tobacco, take a big deep drag, and toddle off to the den to read.

Nathan has every right to quote the same verse back to you. And a sensitive grandpa will listen.

• Express joy in obeying God's Word.

Tom Sawyer was right, you know. If you make something seem fun, others are going to want to do it also. But you have an advantage over Tom. Obeying God's Word brings a lot more pleasure than painting a fence.

Jesus says, "My yoke is easy, and My load is light" (Matthew 11:30). God's Word isn't a burden that we drag around in agony. But, rather, it's a life-style that fits well on us.

If you're known as Kevin's grumpy, complaining, Christian grandmother, it won't motivate many.

"But," you retort, "the Christian life just isn't always happy!"

No, but it can be a life filled with "love, joy, peace, patience, kindness, goodness, faithfulness, gentleness, and self-control" (Galatians 5:22-23).

Let them see you as someone who is still growing, still trying to become the person God wants you to be.

It's not that kids view the grandparents as always perfect. What they most often see is one who refuses to change.

"Grandpa always complains about the preacher's sermon. That's just the way he is," they say.

"Grandma's had that habit since she was a little girl, and there's no way she can stop it now."

Some say it's the privilege of old age. You want to get your life organized. You want everything to be predictable. You are tired of surprises. So you lock in your actions, your environment, and your attitudes. You hunker down in your bunker of life, fighting off any who would try to budge you from what you consider your well-earned position.

But a life of faith isn't that way. Paul never settled down in his faith: "But one thing I do: forgetting what lies behind and reaching forward to what lies ahead, I press on toward the goal for the prize of the upward call of God in Christ Jesus" (Philippians 3:13-14).

Grandkids need to see that the world is not divided into a power system where the older rule the younger and the only chance to change sides is to live long enough. We are all in the same place, no matter what the age, striving to please God and be obedient to Him. Discipline of grandchildren will be more authentic if they see us as fellow learners.

Little Herbie is having a terrible time playing with your neighbor's son. Herbie keeps grabbing the Dudleys' toys and bringing them into your house.

"But I can't help it, Grandpa! I really like that red truck!"

As you give him the pep talk about respecting other's possessions and not letting our desires to have what belongs to others control us, tell him how you struggle in a similar way. Tell him about the little gray beach house up on Cypress Point that you've wanted for twenty-five years. How you used to pray and pray that the Lord would take it away from the owners and give it to you. Tell him how hard it is to realize that you will never have the house, but you've just had to learn that God is in control of things like that and you're learning to be content with what you have.

The sign on the car bumper read: "Grandkids are so much fun, we should have had them first."

Delightful grandchildren are a joy.

Disobedient grandchildren are a pain.

You might not be able to change the disobedient into the delightful in one weekend, but you can make progress.

Shelly sat at the table in her grandmother's kitchen. Her eyes brightened as we entered the room. She seemed pleased that the speakers at church were now going to have dinner with her grandmother, grandfather, and her.

She propped her hands under her chin. "My name's Shelly, and I'll be nine years old on December twenty-fifth, and don't you dare say 'poor thing' because I rather enjoy having my birthday on Christmas."

Caught off guard, we stared in surprise at the girl.

"Well," she announced, "don't mind me. I'm impossible to live with, you know."

"You are?" we stammered.

"Why, yes. My mother tells me that all the time. If I were you I wouldn't eat any of the peas. Grandmother burnt them and then tried to hide it by melting garlic butter on top. Didn't you, Grandmother?"

The entire meal was dominated by one precocious little girl.

"We keep her quite often," the grandmother later confessed. "Her mom and dad are going through a divorce and neither seem in too much of a hurry to have Shelly."

For almost nine years she has had little concern shown her unless she forced her way into the situation. Now, for a short visit every month or so, Grandma and Grandpa would try to teach loving discipline.

A year later we saw Shelly again.

"Are you still quite impossible to live with?" we asked with a laugh.

"Of course!" she snapped back. "But I suppose Grandmother has domesticated me to some small degree."

We shook our heads in amazement.

Later, when Shelly was outside riding a horse, her grandparents explained.

"We've had Shelly a lot this year. And she's still a handful. But she has made several close friends at school, for the first time in her whole life."

"And," Grandmother continued, "she hasn't griped about my cooking for over three months. That's definitely an improvement."

Some might conclude that's not much progress.

But it's not bad for grandparents who only see a grandchild on occasion. It is possible to influence them and still keep them loving you in the process.

That's what good grandparenting is all about.

11

How to Spend a Vacation Together . . . and Not Be Worn to a Frazzle

"**W**hat is your favorite memory of your grandparents?"

We asked that question to dozens and dozens of grandchildren, and we expected a multitude of different answers. In fact, we were counting on a long list that would give us a source of ideas to share with you in this book.

What we found out is that almost every response to that question began with these words: "I remember one vacation being at my grandparents' house . . . "

Every time.

The kids are going to remember the vacations most of all.

"I loved vacations at Grandma's. I always had a great big bed, and a room all to myself!"

"Vacations were the best. Grandpa would take me down to the playground every day."

"You know what my grannie would do? She would fix biscuits and gravy for breakfast any day I asked. I guess in the olden days people really liked to cook."

"Listen, when I went to their house on vacation, I would ride the electric bus downtown with Grandpa. And those buildings were as tall as mountains. We went into this big store, and there was a man with a uniform who held it open for us. I remember he said, 'Good morning, Mr. Temple.' I was impressed that he knew my grandfather's name. Wow, that was my first trip to a big city. It was some vacation."

"My grandad ran this little grocery store on the border of Kansas and Oklahoma, and I'd spend a week or two out there each summer. He'd sit me up on a box behind the counter and let me operate the cash register. There was no greater thrill during those first twelve years of my life. I thought those days would never end."

"Grandma always let me do fancy things when I went to her house. She'd get out her best silver tea service and then we would bake a plate of fancy little cookies. After that we would dress up in our best dresses and just the two of us have tea. I bet it looked kind of silly, but I'll never forget those days as long as I live."

"My grandpa was a quiet, hardworking man. He didn't relax and joke very often. He always seemed so serious. But I loved going to the farm. The summer I was thirteen I stayed for a whole month, and he taught me how to train horses. I think he enjoyed it as much as I did. When it was time to go, he hugged me and I saw tears rolling down his eyes. It was the only time I ever saw him cry."

The stories just go on and on.

There is a love relationship between grandkids and vacations at Grandma and Grandpa's.

How to Make Their Stay a Real Vacation

SET ASIDE TIME TO DO IT RIGHT

If you are not yet retired you will want to make arrangements for your vacation time to blend with your grandchildren's. This will probably mean some advance planning.

You might say, "Well, Grandma's at home with the grandkids, so I'll go ahead and work."

Sure, if there is absolutely no other alternative. But taking away time from the grandkids is not a whole lot different from stealing money from their piggy bank. You are taking something away from them that can never be replaced.

If you see your grandchildren quite often, then perhaps you should go ahead and work. If you see them very seldom, then take your vacation time with them. What are you saving it for?

Many grandparents are retired, or have more flexibility in their schedules, so you will find it easier to arrange your schedule.

Did you ever wonder what your eulogies will sound like? What will the family say when they stand around your grave? A lot of memories are going to start out, "Do you remember that time we spent a week at Grandma and Grandpa's?" Those are the very memories you will build on a vacation with your grandchildren. For the most part, you will be remembered as you were during those few short days together.

How much time do you need to do it right?

Some folks recommend one day for each year they are old. Have the three-year-old stay for three days, the six-year-old for six days, and the ten-year-old ten days, and so on. But all of that varies depending on time, distance, health, money, and so forth.

Aim for one whole week. That will give you time to do a variety of weekday and weekend activities, including attending worship together.

If, for some reason, your grandchildren's parents just can't afford to send the kids to your house, do whatever you can to help with the costs. "But," you explain, "they live clear across the country." In that case, you probably haven't had the opportunity to spend very much on them, so this will be a good time to catch up.

Perhaps you had the idea to leave each of the grandkids a couple thousand dollars' inheritance. It would be better to invest in airline tickets while you are still around. The impact will be far greater and more lasting.

FOCUS YOUR ENTIRE TIME ON YOUR GRANDCHILD

Yes, there might be an occasional circumstance where this is impossible. But set it as your goal. Cancel your weekly golf game. Reschedule the art class. Replace the shock absorbers on the car some other week. Paint the garage next summer. Host the women's Bible study next month. Give this time to your grandchildren.

Such single-mindedness makes a statement about yourself. It lets others know, in a helpful way, what is really important in your life.

It also might be the only time in the child's life when he commands the undivided attention of an adult. Mom visits with him while she cooks dinner and drives him to band practice. Dad visits over the top of the newspaper or during TV commercials.

Sure, Dad plays catch, but he only has a few minutes after dinner and before he has to run to another meeting. Mom wants to look at all the doll clothes but has to hurry to get herself ready for work every morning.

Grandma and Grandpa?

One small boy wrote. "I don't think my grandma and grandpa have very many friends. When I go to visit them, they don't have anyone to talk to but me. They never seem to have anywhere to go. They just want to play. It must be fun to be a grandparent. I think I'll be a grandfather when I am very, very old."

ARRANGE THE TIMING OF THEIR VISIT

You will need to consider . . .

- The season of the year.

If you live in Florida, the summer might be too hot and sweltering for a boy from Colorado. If you live in Minnesota, perhaps January is too cold for your Arizona granddaughter. Or the extreme change might be an added attraction. The point is, carefully think through which season would best fit this particular child.

- The age of the child.

The twelve-year-old will love swimming in the lake, but that only happens in July and August. The five-year-old is afraid of water, so it doesn't matter if he comes during the swimming season. Your sixteen-year-old will have cheerleading practice in August, so you'd better schedule something in early summer.

- The interests of the child.

John likes to water ski, so ask him to come in July. Trinka loves to downhill ski; invite her during Christmas break. Ronnie likes to fish. You might ask him to come in early June, when the water is high and the fish are big. Little Sarae loves to see the animals in the zoo. How about Easter for her? And Geoffry? If there are cookies he'll come any day of the year.

- The activities in your area.

If your grandson, Martin, is an avid baseball fan, invite him to your place in Phoenix in March when spring training is in bloom. If you have a big boat show coming up in August, ask your granddaughter, Crystal, who loves races. When the Shakespeare festival hits town, have Lisa, your actress, come visit.

Any old week would be good for a visit, but some weeks will be better than others.

INVITE YOUR GRANDKIDS TO COME VISIT ONE AT A TIME

OK, it might be totally impossible.

But try . . . try . . . try.

The more grandkids you have, the more they need a time to be by themselves. If you have to bunch them up, then how about a couple of compatible cousins instead of brothers?

Why have them one at a time?

- Because it might be the only time during the year that they get a break from their family, and their family from them.
- Because it gives them a short chance to seek their individual identity, apart from the others.
- Because it will help you get to know each as a person, not one of a larger group.
- Because most kids act better (during a visit) without the family pecking order. There is no little brother to fight with or big sister who is trying to borrow clothes.
- Because when you are dealing with them only one at a time you can insure they each have fun. Jannie loves Chinese food. Lannie hates it. Lannie loves Italian food. Jannie hates it. When you have them both over, where do you eat out? At the Taco Joint. But when you have them one at a time? Each is delighted to get to choose the restaurant on her own.
- Because, for many, it is their first attempt to survive apart from their parents, and you will be right there to help them. They may not want a brother or sister witnessing this struggle.

The most precious memories we heard about from grandkids involved "just me and my grandma," or "just me and Grandpa." "It's no exaggeration. When we were kids, the most exciting time of the year was our individual trips to Grandma and Grandpa's house. I think we felt as though we had each won the lottery. I can still remember the feeling of seeing my sisters stare out the back window of our family car as they drove away. They always looked like puppies going to the pound. I felt so proud, I wanted to salute."

KNOW AHEAD OF TIME ALL THE ACTIVITIES IN YOUR AREA FOR KIDS THEIR AGE

This information is not too hard to find out. Ask some of the kids at church what are the most fun things to do in town.

Ask them . . .

- "Where is your favorite place to eat out?"
  (Remember there are pizza joints, and there is *the* pizza joint.)
- "Where's the most fun store to shop?"
  (At age twelve it just might not be Grandma's favorite department store downtown.)
- "If you had an afternoon to do anything in this area you wanted, what would it be?"
  (And you didn't even know that there was a water slide over next to the river, did you?)
- "Which park has the best toys?"
  (That nice park just down from your house might not have the most awesome swings and radical slides.)

Call your local Chamber of Commerce to find out upcoming activities. You might not know everything that's going on. A car show at the mall. A concert at the civic auditorium. A circus at the fairgrounds. Or how about a bike ride along the levy?

When your ten-year-old bursts through the door with, "What's happenin', Grandma?" You'll know how to answer him better than anyone else in town.

DON'T FORGET THE HISTORICAL POINTS
OF INTEREST AROUND YOUR AREA

They might be so common that you forget what's there. Again, the Chamber of Commerce or your county historical society might have some maps that show the highlights.

We love living in northern Idaho. You might not think too much has happened up here. You've probably never heard of towns like Winchester, Weippe, Grangeville, and Dixie.

Yet, just down the hill a few miles from our house is the Clearwater River. Lewis and Clark floated down that very spot in 1805. Not far southeast of our house the Nez Percé Indian War began in 1877. It is considered one of the most masterful military retreats in history. Only twenty-five miles from our front door is the lower entrance to Hell's Canyon, the deepest gorge in our country. Up on the other side of the Clearwater stand the ruins of the first gold mine discovered in what is now Idaho, and not too far from it you can find old prospectors still digging for gold. We live just south of the Palouse region where Appaloosa horses (famous for the spots on their rumps) originated.

But our home's not in an extraordinary location. There are exciting points of history and geography in every region.

So scout around. Find out . . .

- how to get there
- the best time of the day to be there
- any costs that are involved
- how much time it takes to view the site
- how long it will take to drive there and back
- if there is any place to eat when you get there

Teach your grandchildren local history.

Now, some of your grandkids will not seem in the least interested. However, you don't have to ask them if they want to go—just take them. Kids seldom have an accurate view of the importance of things. But the day will come when it all comes back and they say, "Hey, I once went there with my grandparents!"

"Well," you say, "that sounds like a very intense and tiring week."

Sure. Isn't that the reason you have been eating oat bran and wheat germ all year? Just why is it you want to live long and be strong and healthy? "So I'll be able to enjoy the family more," you have stated.

All right . . . get ready . . . here come the grandkids.

Traveling with Grandkids

Now, what about those grandparents who are still working? Or the ones who just don't have facilities for grandkids in their home? Or the grandparents who love to travel and are almost always on the road? The solution? Take the grandkids on vacation with you.

Many of the home rules given in earlier chapters still apply.

1. *Remember the days = years formula given earlier in the chapter.* Four-year-olds travel for four days, eight-year-olds for eight, and so on.
2. *Make sure your travel vehicle fits the child.* Don't cram four grandkids in the back seat of a compact car for a five-hundred-mile trip.
3. *Take them one at a time if possible.* How about as a present on each of their twelfth birthdays? Or tenth? Or eighth?
4. *Know your highways.* Will it be mountainous roads? Freeways? Unpaved? (Yep, there are still plenty of them in our country.)
5. *Know the history of the region.* Read up ahead of time and give your grandkids a running commentary of what happened where and when.
6. *Grab a notebook to record the animals, fauna, flowers, and geography you will view.* Stop and show them the difference between pine, fir, and cedar trees. Walk along the beach and collect the shells. Then identify each one.
7. *Know the endurance of the kids.* How many miles before a potty stop? A fast food break? A playground?
8. *Have some ideas for conversations and games as you travel.* A whole industry flourishes by producing car games for kids. Ask at your nearest toy store, and check at the book store. But the best games will be the ones you invent along the way.

9. *Keep some exciting destination just up ahead.* Yellowstone, Cody, Cheyenne, Denver, Santa Fe, Las Cruces, Tombstone, Phoenix, Grand Canyon, Monument Valley, Telluride . . . .

10. *Let them make some of the decisions.* Will it be McDonald's or Burger King? Will you stay the night at The Riverview or at The Silver Palace? Will you visit the modern art museum or the miniature golf course?

11. *Challenge them to new experiences.* Help them climb to the top of a volcano. Raft down the river. Ride on the stern wheeler. Dine in the fancy restaurant. Hike across the Civil War battlefield. Sail on a boat across the harbor. Sample the entries in the chili cook-off. Watch the Indian tribal dance.

12. *Give them a break from the grind of travel.* In the middle of the week, stay an extra day in one place so they (and you) can rest up. Stop at a city park every few hours and let them run around for a while. Get to a motel early enough for them to swim, or play catch, and unwind.

13. *Look for points of spiritual interest as well.* Show them the tabernacle where Billy Sunday once preached. Drive by the famous 10,000-member church. Visit the campuses of Christian colleges, even when the grandkids are young, to give them some future possibilities.

"OK," you sigh, "but where should we take them?"

That all depends upon money, time, and desire. But we suggest looking for something different.

If they live in a city, take them to a farm in the country.

If they live in the country, take them to a big city.

If they live by the ocean, take them to the desert.

If they live on the plains, take them to the mountains.

Check out national parks, adjoining states, neighboring foreign countries, state capitals, famous resort areas, and remote, secluded coves.

Most kids will like any place as long as Grandma and Grandpa are there.

Ask yourself, "Where did I want to go when I was their age?" Did you ever make it? Did they? If not, why not make this the year you finally go?

But don't forget their spiritual life as you travel. It's a good time to read some verses together each morning and pray for the Lord's safety and leading. It will be natural to take time in the evening to thank God for the events of the day. Point out God's handiwork as you travel along. Find a good church and attend Sunday school and worship together. Help them to know that God travels with them at all times.

What will the grandkids gain by being with you on vacation?

- They will gain a closeness to their grandparents. Shared new experiences sink deep in the memory.
- They will become more creative. Traveling stimulates the mind.
- They will gain more ideas for their future by seeing a big, wide world.
- They will have time to miss their family and their normal routine.

What will the children's parents gain by your taking the kids on vacation?

- About three hours of sleep every night!
- Some time to work more closely on relationships with the other children or each other.
- An example for them to copy in future years.
- A time to really miss the child (or children).

What will you gain by taking them with you on vacation?

- New respect for what it is like to be a kid in today's world.
- The delightful joy of seeing the world through a kid's eyes once again.
- An understanding for the job their parents face.
- About two hundred hugs and a couple dozen smooches on the cheek. (Which, in themselves, should be reward enough.)

Steve spent most of his childhood years living across the street from one set of grandparents and two doors away from the other.

"Hardly a day would go by that I wasn't in the house of one set or the other, or both. I played games, sang songs, ate meals (lots of meals), and visited with both sides constantly.

"But they have all been gone over twenty years now. And my memory of them is beginning to fade. If you asked me to tell you all about them, well, I'd have some trouble . . . especially on the Bly side. Grandma and Grandpa were people of the land. Their hard-earned farm took most of their attention. They seldom traveled anywhere away from it. But I do remember my grandmother a little better than my grandfather. You see, two different times Grandmother took me on a vacation with her. I remember both of those trips.

"Now, on the other side of the family, I have plenty of fond memories still. You see, every summer, for years, I traveled to the coast with my Grandma and Grandpa Wilson. So I have a memory still chock full of featherbeds and fireworks, tom cods and halibuts, boardwalks and the penny arcades. We would stop at Tiny's for breakfast and a place that served artichoke milk shakes for lunch. And sometimes during the course of the week we would cruise along the Seventeen Mile Drive to see how the rich folks lived.

"I remember it all. From Grandpa's deep laugh to Grandma's warm hug.

"I was just a kid then.

"A kid on vacation.

"A kid on vacation with Grandma and Grandpa."

There are some things you never forget.

12

How Any Grandparent Can Be the World's Best Baby-sitter

The tanned couple sat down next to us for dinner at a conference in Arizona. The conversation turned from the weather, to children, then to grandchildren. The question popped up, "Are grandparents good baby-sitters?"

"We can't help you there," the man replied. "We only have one child. She and her family live in Montana, so we don't really get a chance to baby-sit."

"Oh, that's too bad," we consoled. "How about when you raised your own daughter? Did you find that your parents made good baby-sitters?"

"They never baby-sat. We weren't going to leave our little Julia with anyone else. We never did have a baby-sitter, ever. If we couldn't take her along, we just didn't go."

"You never had a baby-sitter?" we gasped.

"Nope."

Then his wife entered in, "Well, there was just one time that my mother watched her for an hour or so . . . "

Then he boomed back, "But that was it. No sir, we weren't going to let someone else raise our kid."

Their "kid" is now forty-seven years old. How we wanted to hear the story from her point of view.

But that family is an extreme, we hope.

Bud and Cleo rejoiced when Danny, Margie, and the boys moved back to town. It was going to be great to have the children and grandchildren live right on the same block. No more driving six hours through the desert to get to their house.

The grandkids spent most of the summer in Bud and Cleo's swimming pool, which gave their folks some time to get unpacked and move in. When school started in the fall, the schedule changed—a little.

Margie decided to finish college, so this meant going to school on Tuesdays and Thursdays. Well, Cleo thought she could surely babysit a couple days a week, even though Bud was still working long hours.

She hadn't counted on Margie's night school class and Danny's bowling league on Tuesday nights. Sometimes the boys just spent the night at Grandma and Grandpa's. When the second semester rolled around the school schedule was shifted to Monday, Wednesday, and Friday. And this year, Margie decided to take classes five days a week until she graduates. Now she hints about going to graduate school.

Bud and Cleo dearly love their kids and their grandkids. But they're plumb worn out. They hate to admit that, so they struggle along, trying to endure.

Their situation is an extreme—we hope.

Most of the rest of us fit somewhere in between.

In surveying parents across the country, there is a near unanimous consensus that leaving the kids with the grandparents is the next best thing to being with them yourself. And in some cases, it's even better.

WHY PARENTS LIKE GRANDPARENT BABY-SITTERS

They have years of experience.

Thirteen-year-old girls can make terrific baby-sitters. But you worry a bit at their inexperience. What if Waldo throws up all over the sofa? What if Belinda cuts her finger? What if some irate stranger appears at the front door? What if little Uriah tries that "I'm going to hold my breath until I get my way" trick? Grandmother and Grandfather have been through it all. "If they can raise a kid like me," the parents reason, "then they can do anything."

They have a preestablished relationship with the children.
Your best friend at church tells you about this lady who's new in town and really a good baby-sitter. Mature, experienced, caring. But she doesn't know little Antoinette. Your daughter is extremely shy at meeting new people. Often she won't even speak a word the whole evening. A baby-sitter has to be really sensitive with her.

So Mom turns to Antoinette's grandparents. Antoinette dearly loves to go to Grandpa and Grandma's. They seem to know how to draw her out of her shell. She'll go with them places even her parents can't get her to go.

They have ownership in the children.
Other folks, no matter how caring, don't have blood ties to these children. For some, baby-sitting is just a job. There is no reason to get too personal. For others, they sincerely pay attention to the children—but only during the time they are together.

Grandparents are different. They care about the kids all the time. Their world seems to rotate around those little ones. They know what Leopold likes to eat, and what he wants for a birthday present, and why it is he had a rotten day at school last Tuesday.

Grandparents care about who they are, how they feel, what they want to be when they grow up, who they will someday marry, how they feel about themselves, and whether their socks match.

They provide a familiar environment for the children.
Grandparents can come to the kids' house and know the routine. You don't have to tell them where you keep the emergency ration of cookies, or where the dryer is in case Nigel doesn't have clean jammies, or where to find bandages for Henrietta's skinned-up knee. Besides, Grandmas are noted for washing the dishes, cycling a couple of loads of clothes, and vacuuming the living room before Mom and Dad back out of the driveway. Grandpas seem to delight in replacing light bulbs, fixing screen doors, watering the dry lawn, and inventing a little dorwadjit that keeps a dishwasher from plugging up so often.

If the kids are brought to Grandma and Grandpa's house, there's a bigger advantage for parents (like not having to clean the house). It's a familiar place for the kids. They already know where the toys are stored, what rooms are off limits, and exactly where Grandma's cookie jar is (and it never seems to have store-bought cookies like the one at home).

Grandparents need little supervision from the parents.

A grandparent doesn't need to be called halfway through the evening to see if all is well. And the parents won't receive a desperation call either. There's no need to give them the phone number of a doctor, the nearest hospital, a neighbor, a lawyer, and above all else, a plumber. Somehow they'll survive on their own.

No list is needed of what Crissy won't eat or what Mason needs to wear to bed. It's the one place the kids can be let off at the curb, with Grandpa standing in the doorway, and not have another worry.

Besides all this, grandparents are inexpensive.

To be honest, this is a great delight to parents. The amount saved for baby-sitting can pay for dinner.

A few years back we ran a program at church of free baby-sitting one Friday night per month. We wanted to strengthen husband and wife relationships and felt every couple deserved one night a month to themselves. It was a huge success.

Several wives told us that it was the first time since the children were born that they had been out on a date alone with hubby. "It's too hard to get good sitters," one said, "and Barry says we really can't afford it." Without fail, those who took advantage of the program most were families whose grandparents lived far away.

Never underestimate the attraction of free baby-sitting.

KIDS ENJOY GRANDPARENT BABY-SITTERS

Kids are free to be themselves.

In a new relationship there's a lot of awkward time just trying to find out what the baby-sitter is like and what they expect and how one should act. With Grandma the child's not afraid to giggle, or cheer at the ball game on television, or run around in his underwear. "It's just Grandma and Grandpa, and they like me the way I am!"

Kids feel loved.
Even animals can sense when they are truly loved. How much more can children. "Grandma might not feel good, and Grandpa might be tired, but they still love me."

They get undivided attention.
"I went to my grandma's last night," one little girl told us, "and we were playing a game when the phone rang. Well, she answered it and said, 'I'm sorry, I'm busy playing a game with my granddaughter, you'll just have to call back tomorrow.' Grandma really likes to play games with me."

Kids feel secure with Grandpa and Grandma.
"We had a big lightning storm last night, but my grandpa was baby-sitting. So he lit some candles, and we sat on the couch next to him, and he told stories about when he was camping out in the woods for a whole summer and never had any electricity. He let us stay right there until the lights came on again. My grandpa isn't afraid of anything!"

Kids enjoy getting spoiled.
They indulge in cookies and ice cream (sometimes right before dinner!). "And Grandpa takes us down to the mall for a walk and usually buys us a toy. And they let me stay up until almost nine. Grandma always fixes too much food, so I'm supposed to eat a lot. Grandpa takes me out into the shop and lets me use his tools. Boy, if I couldn't live at home, I would sure want to live with my grandma and grandpa."

Grandparents have this habit of buying things, making things, giving away things. Grandkids love it.

In most cases, the only problem the kids have with the grandparents baby-sitting is facing the reality of leaving.

WHY GRANDPARENTS SOMETIMES HATE TO BABY-SIT

If parents love it, and kids love it, why is it grandparents sometimes hate to baby-sit?

Let's face it. Baby-sitting is not always a piece of cake. Sometimes it is a pain. What causes the problems?

Perhaps it's because of physical limitations.

There is a good reason why the prime child-bearing years are eighteen to twenty-eight. No matter how great a shape you try to maintain, sixty is not thirty. And seventy is nowhere near forty. On top of that, if you develop weak knees, a bum back, stiffened joints, or any of those other lovely signs of aging, certain aspects of grandparenting spell physical agony.

All of this produces a mental strain as well, because you would like to have the stamina to keep the kids more. So you, too, look forward to their every visit but sigh with relief when they leave.

At times, grandparenting is tough because parents have not taught their kids any discipline or respect.

This is a hard problem to admit. Some grandkids are difficult to handle. They refuse to mind you, reject your correction, destroy your belongings, bother the neighbors, embarrass you in public, and act like you owe them something. You can blame them, or you can blame their parents. Either way, you face a tough situation. Most of the times you don't have them long enough to make much impact in changing them.

The best you can do is brace yourself for a human hurricane and hope that it passes through quickly.

Baby-sitting can be rough because grandparents are not always told the rules of the game.

For whatever reason, mothers have been known to assume that grandparents know more than they do. You feed Ethan chocolate cake, and your daughter criticizes you for giving him chocolate. You allow Yolanda to watch a cartoon show until nine, and your son berates you for not putting her to bed at eight-thirty. You allow Jasmine to call her friends on the phone, and then find out her parents never want her to call that guy again.

Nobody told you the rules until after you'd broken them. It's easy to get gun-shy.

Sometimes grandparents just aren't equipped to handle the particular situation.

They bring the two-year-old, Bertram, but never the high chair. So you have to sit at the table holding a Jello tossing, spinach spitting, squirm-bomb in your lap while you grab a bite to eat.

Melinda is supposed to practice her cheerleading in your living room, but you live in a condo with a mean looking couple lurking in the unit under yours.

You're asked to help Dexter with his homework, but you don't have the foggiest notion how to do precalculus.

Lack of adequate advance notices make grandparenting a strain.

"Oh, Mom, glad we caught you at home. Jerry just called and wants me to meet him downtown. Hope you can keep the kids. Give Stanley a bath, and Shirley needs her hair washed, and take a look at Sammy's hand—I don't think he'll need stitches. We'll try to get back by twelve thirty or one, but if it's going to be later, we'll call . . . have fun!"

Fun?

Some grandparents have struggles because of unresolved differences with the parents of the grandchildren.

Your daughter-in-law thinks you are far too strict with the grandchildren and has often told you so. Yet, your son keeps bringing them over to spend the evening. So you feel tense the whole evening wondering what you should do and say to make everyone happy. But your tenseness makes the kids act up, which doubles your anxiety.

Fortunately, this isn't always the case. Nor should it be. We can, and should, try to build a base where the children will be welcomed and well cared for.

We have no idea if Jesus ever had the joy of baby-sitting His younger brothers and sisters. But He never seemed to mind the interruptions of children.

> And they were bringing children to Him so that He might touch them; and the disciples rebuked them. But when Jesus saw this, He was indignant and said to them, "Permit the children to come to Me; do not hinder them; for the kingdom of God belongs to such as these. Truly I say to you, whoever does not receive the

kingdom of God like a child shall not enter it at all." And He took them in His arms and began blessing them, laying His hands upon them. (Mark 10:13-16)

Perhaps that line "Permit the children to come to me . . . " should be a grandparent's theme verse.

So how can we make that happen in the best possible way?

Develop a Basic Baby-sitting Strategy

Kid-proof your house.

No, don't sell your furniture and trade the china for Melmac. Just walk around and look for places where you are asking for trouble. Check out little rugs that slip . . . glass figurines perched on low coffee tables . . . fireplace matches on the hearth instead of the mantel . . . chairs too frail for a six-year-old's jumps (and they must jump, you know). Scout the yard as well. Undefined flower beds can easily turn into end zones for football games. Garden tools can injure little hands. And mud holes will be instantly discovered no matter how cleverly disguised.

You don't want to spend the entire time yelling, "No! Don't touch that!" So make changes that will smooth the relationship.

Purchase some necessary items.

All this will depend upon your budget. If things are tight you will be surprised at the quality goods you can discover with some careful "thrift store" shopping.

You might need your own highchair, playpen, or crib. Consider a swing for your backyard, a basketball hoop on the garage, an extension phone in the den. You'll probably need a video machine, a well-stocked game chest, and the latest equivalent of Lincoln Logs.

By all means, if you have a stereo, buy a very nice set of headphones, which will assure you that you will not have to listen to all the music. In fact, buy two sets of headphones and a little attachment to use them both at the same time. That way your grandchild can share his latest tape with a friend.

Build a guardrail on the bed. Stretch an expandable gate across the stairs. Invest in cute plastic picnic dishes for their dinnerware.

Own at least one stretch-out-and-put-your-feet-on couch and a bed-spread that can be tossed in the machine and washed when decorated with spaghetti sauce.

Pile up the pantry.

A good supply of nonperishables will always come in handy—some of their favorite soups, packages of chocolate mix, a few of those horrid little squiggly noodles and tasteless meatballs they love, and, of course, the world's favorite . . . macaroni and cheese.

If you've followed the suggestions earlier in the book you'll have a list of each one's favorite food items. If you didn't get a chance to purchase them before they arrived, load them into the car and hit the supermarket first thing.

Bake a favorite goodie, too. Homemade treats not only taste better; you're preserving history. Some kids would never know what a real cake tasted like if Grandma didn't bake one.

Ask some basic questions.

Every time the grandkids are dropped off, check on the specific bedtimes. Tell Mom what you were planning to feed them and get her approval. Find out the evening's "dos and don'ts." Ask about television programs, bedtime wear, and rules for using the telephone.

Volunteer before you're asked.

If you always volunteer, then the children's parents will know for sure you want to baby-sit, and you can be specific about which times you're available. If, for example, you and your mate attend a home Bible study every Wednesday night, then volunteer for "any night except Wednesday." You can say, "We'd love to baby-sit once a week!" . . . which also says more often than that might be too much.

Learn how to say no.

It would be best if your kids only asked you to baby-sit at convenient times. But there are times when it's not. You must say no.

But always explain your reasons. "Grandpa's sick." "I've got to work tonight." "We have some other plans."

Then offer to help them find a sitter. "I'll call someone from the church." Or, "I'll check with my neighbor's daughter."

If you can, volunteer for your next available time. "I'm sorry, honey, but we can't do it on Friday. We'd be happy to have the kids on Saturday, though."

Make sure they all know your rules.

Parents and grandkids both need to know the rules of your house and understand them.

But don't forget, you need some rules as well. Grandparents have to toe the line at times, just like the parents and grandchildren. So here are a few suggestions:

BABY-SITTING NO-NO'S

- Never put down, subtly or overtly, implied or stated, the principles and/or rules of the grandchildren's mother or father.
- Never argue with your mate in front of the grandchildren.
- Never put down another of the grandchildren in front of the others.
- Never abandon a child in front of the television set. Make sure you control what is watched—whether network, cable, movie videos, or games.
- Never knowingly fill the children with fear (recounting violent news accounts, telling scary stories, and so on).
- Never forget the long-range health of the children when deciding what they should eat.

These can give you some ideas, and perhaps you and your mate will want to add to your list of guidelines.

"Who's your favorite baby-sitter?" we recently asked nine-year-old William.

"My grandma!" he shot back.

"Why do you like her best?"

"Because I get things," he smiled.

"What kind of things?"

"Oh, baseball cards, and cars, and ice cream, and homemade custard. Besides that, I get to play with Alvin."

"Alvin?"

"Grandmother's teddy bear. No one can touch him but me and her."

"So you like being there because you get lots of things?"

"Yep. And besides that, she's nice."

"Er . . . she's nice? What does that mean?"

"She likes me, and she doesn't yell, and she won't bite me."

"Do some people not like you?"

"Sure. But Grandma likes me even if I'm naughty."

"Are you naughty very often?"

"Nope. But even if I was, Grandma would still let me stay at her house. I had a dream about her house last night."

"You did? What was it about?"

"Well, it was real scary. I was lost, and I couldn't find my house. I mean, it wasn't on the right street, and there were some dogs chasing me and trying to eat me."

"Wow! What did you do, William?"

"Oh, I just ran to Grandma's house, and she let me in."

"Even though the dogs were chasing you?"

"Oh, sure. That's the way grandmas are, you know."

We know.
Grandparents make great baby-sitters.

13

How to Pray for Your Grandchildren

"We won't see our grandkids for five more years!"

Gary and Beverly are parents of missionaries. That means their grandchildren are MKs. They will grow up in a remote area of Paraguay. Jacob is ten, Julie seven, and Justin three. When they next see Grandma and Grandpa they will be fifteen, twelve, and eight, speak Spanish more fluently than English, and feel culturally out of place in the United States.

So, how can Gary and Beverly act as good grandparents?

They can make sure that the kids have what they need more than anything else in the world—prayer.

Your grandkids live clear across the country? Or broken relationships and divorce make it impossible for you to even see them? Perhaps they are all grown and gone their separate ways, seldom making contact with you. What is your responsibility in such cases?

The primary function of grandparenting, whether they live across the street or around the globe—whether you see them every day or once in every ten years—remains the same: pray for your grandkids.

But they need more than just an occasional "Bless the grandchildren, Lord." Here are some ideas for establishing an effective prayer ministry for your grandchildren.

GRANDPARENTS WHO ARE SERIOUS ABOUT PRAYER

MAKE A PICTURE PRAYER JOURNAL FOR EACH OF THE GRANDKIDS

This picture prayer journal should be a working document, not a keepsake album. Make something simple, portable, and replaceable.

We suggest using an eighty-nine-cent stenographer's pad (the kind you can pick up at your supermarket). Then make a list of your grandchildren, beginning with the oldest and right down to the baby. Using a page for each grandchild, write the child's full name across the top of the page. Unless you are blessed with seventy-five grandkids, leave a blank page or two in your notebook between grandchildren. That way the notebook will last for a few years before it fills up.

Then, in the upper left-hand corner use a glue stick and paste in the latest picture you have of the grandchild. Those little wallet-size school pictures work well. It should look like this:

[notebook page 1]

Jerome Lee Atwood
July 14, 1978

(photo)

[notebook page 4]

Jessica Lynn Atwood
July 19, 1981

(photo)

Now you're ready to fill up the blank pages with notes and requests. The steno-size book will slip nicely into the back of most Bibles and you can carry it with you and use it as a reminder each time you read your Bible.

Our friend Peggy found she consistently had about ten minutes of quiet time in the sanctuary between the closing of Sunday school and the beginning of the morning service. She uses this as a time of prayer for her grandchildren.

What goes into the prayer journal?

• The ordinary needs of kids.

You will want to jot down requests about their health and safety; mental, physical, and spiritual growth; peer pressure; temptations from sex, drugs, and the like.

• Also, you will want to jot down specific needs.

Every time you get a letter from a grandchild or from their parents, scan for particular needs of the kids.

Things like:

> Terry is worried about making the football team.
> Larry sprained his wrist.
> Gary is having trouble with a kid on the school bus.
> Mary is going to sing a solo in the children's choir.
> Barry thinks his ears are too big.
> Carrie thinks she will die if she doesn't get straight A's.
> Harry will be going to church winter camp.
> Jerry has to have two teeth pulled.
> Perry just broke up with his girlfriend.

If you use a pencil, you can add corrections and updates.

How often do you pray through your entire journal? That depends on your schedule, the number of grandchildren you have, and how many requests you have listed. Certainly once a day is not too often. Once a month, for each one separately, would be the minimum. If you happen to have seven, or fewer, grandchildren, assign each one to a particular day of the week. (Wednesdays pray for Brad, Thursdays for Chad, Fridays for Thad, and so on.)

DEVELOP A MONTHLY PRAYER CALENDAR

Again, we believe in economy. You don't need some expensive, leather bound daily appointment book. Just a little yearly, month-by-month calendar will do—the kind that the drugstores give away for free every Christmas. Make it small enough to fit into your purse, pocket, or Bible.

The first of each year write in all the grandchildren's birthdays.

As you hear of special events or happenings in their lives, jot down the date on your calendar. These are not, necessarily, things that you will attend (those should go on your main calendar). On the days you mark on the prayer calender you will have special prayer for that particular grandchild.

Your calendar will be filled with items like:

April 4:   Faith gets her braces taken off.
April 9:   Felicia's piano recital.
April 16:   Freda's birthday.
April 21:   Felix gets baptized.
April 24:   Floyd takes the college entrance exam.

You will not be told all the events in your grandchildren's lives, but you can be faithful in praying for the ones you know about. Each day, you and your mate can glance at the grandkids' prayer calendar and pray for any special need of that particular day.

We don't need to convince you that prayer is a necessary ingredient for any Christian. You've probably memorized the verses, as we have, such as James 5:16, "The effective prayer of a righteous man can accomplish much." Or how about Matthew 18:19-20? "Again I say to you, that if two of you agree on earth about anything that they may ask, it shall be done for them by My Father who is in heaven. For where two or three have gathered together in My name, there I am in their midst."

Two people in agreement.

It just takes one grandma and one grandpa in prayer to meet the requirements of this verse.

DEVELOP A FEW "HOW TO" PRAYER GUIDES

You will soon discover what particular topics are most important for you as you pray for your grandchildren. The following seven areas can serve as starting points.

Pray for their education.

- that God will give them a desire to do their best.
- that their minds will be challenged.
- for their teachers.
- for the school system they are under.
- that a balance of subjects and ideas will be presented.
- for a safe, healthy classroom environment.
- for them to have the courage to speak biblical truth even in the classroom.
- that they will be learning God's lesson even in nonacademic times.
- that they can learn facts and principles that can later be used in a career that brings God glory.
- that they will learn lessons in life much deeper than report cards and achievement tests can measure.

Pray for their salvation.

"Brethren, my heart's desire and my prayer to God for them is for their salvation," Paul wrote in Romans 10:1.

- that God will bring people into their lives to present the gospel to them.
- that Satan will be kept from blinding them to God's wisdom.
- for the Holy Spirit to reveal spiritual truth to them in a way that leads them to new life in Christ.
- for them to have Christian friends.
- for the church they attend and the people who work with youth their age.
- that they will develop a hunger to read God's Word.
- when you get desperate enough, pray for God to use any means possible to bring them to Himself.

Pray for their future mate.
No matter what the age, pray about who they will someday marry.

- that they, and their future mate, are developing a biblical view of the role of man and woman, husband and wife.
- that they will find a mate who has a growing relationship with Jesus Christ.
- for their future mate to be one who is able to help them achieve God's best.
- that your grandchild will develop a healthy and biblical view of sex.
- that they will have the discipline and moral courage to keep themselves pure for their future mate.
- for their mate to be one who will provide a stable, loving, Christian home for your future great-grandchildren.

Pray for their career.
When they are still growing up, pray . . .

- that they will be interested in seeking God's wisdom about a future vocation.
- that they will find a position that utilizes all of their God-given gifts, talents, and ministries.
- that they might find a life's calling that provides them many spiritual opportunities.
- that some of them will find their life's work in full-time Christian service.
- that those who will be blessed with riches might find satisfaction in using that wealth for the expansion of God's kingdom.

For those who are presently working, pray . . .

- that they, too, will find God's purpose in their everyday labors.
- for them to have the courage to change vocations if they sense God's leading in another direction.
- that they will build a reputation for hard work, loyalty, and honesty.

- that they might be a witness to their co-workers of God's saving power.

Pray for their wisdom.

Paul had this prayer for the people in Ephesus: "[I pray] that the God of our Lord Jesus Christ, the Father of glory, may give to you a spirit of wisdom and of revelation in the knowledge of Him. I pray that the eyes of your heart may be enlightened, so that you may know what is the hope of His calling, what are the riches of the glory of His inheritance in the saints, and what is the surpassing greatness of His power toward us who believe" (Ephesians 1:17-19).

What a wonderful prayer to use for grandchildren.

We don't want our grandkids to merely be the smartest kids in the word—we want them to be the wisest as well. Wisdom is knowing the most godly goal to strive for and the most godly method of achieving that goal. So pray . . . .

- that they will know what to do with their education.
- that they will have self-control in their beauty, charm, and strength.
- that they will know the weaknesses of their own hearts and the wickedness of their own wills.
- for them to learn to trust the Lord's wisdom above their own.

Pray for their trials.

- that the tough times they face might be turned into sources of spiritual good.
- for them not to be overwhelmed with the injustice or the power of evil they face.
- that they will be able to confess their sins.
- that they can quickly work through to a solution that pleases God.
- for them to war effectively against the "rulers, against the powers, against the world forces of this darkness, against the spiritual forces of wickedness in the heavenly places" (Ephesians 6:12).

- for them to have just enough trials to keep their trust completely in God's power and grace.

Pray for their health and safety.
We all want our grandchildren to never get sick, never get hurt, never face any physical pain and struggle. There is nothing wrong in praying for each of these things.

"Beloved, I pray that in all respects you may prosper and be in good health, just as your soul prospers" (3 John 2).

But, our grandchildren will face some of these problems. Just keep praying . . .

- for God to heal your grandchildren. God has the power to do whatever He chooses, and their healing is heavy on your heart.
- for their parents to be able to make the right treatment decisions.
- for the doctors to have the medical knowledge to deal with this situation.
- for God to get glory and honor and praise, in spite of a health problem.
- for your grandchildren to develop a life-style that is healthy, one that will prevent them from suffering many infirmities.
- for their safety—at home, and in the neighborhood, and at school, and on the job.
- for them to sense God's presence during the scary times.
- for them to have the strength of spirit to overcome the fear that Satan will try to bring into their lives.

Let them know you are praying for them.
Never underestimate the power of Grandma and Grandpa's prayers. Just the knowledge that you are praying will act as a loving reminder.

We sat in the bleachers waiting for a football game to begin. A row of college girls sat behind us. We couldn't help listening in.

"Tricia! Wow, you're home! How was Italy?"
"It is totally, totally, totally— mega-awesome."
"Oh, yeah? How about the boys?"

"That's what I was talking about."

"Oh! Did you have a lot of dates—and stuff?"

"Plenty of dates—but no 'stuff.'"

"Are the guys, kind of—weird?"

"No, they were all very smooth."

"All right! But, you didn't even . . . "

"I didn't even let them kiss me."

"Really? Why not?"

"I was only there two weeks! Besides, my grandmother kept putting the pressure on me to behave."

"Your grandmother? You went to Italy with your grandmother?"

"Nah. She lives in a little apartment in Los Angeles."

"Well, how did she . . . ?"

"See, on the day I left for Europe she sent me this little card with some money for the trip and a note that said, 'Tricia, I know you'll have a great time; I'll be praying for you every day.'"

"Yeah, so what?"

"Well, when my granny says she'll be praying, she really means it. She's the type that gets down on her knees and really prays. So, I'm over in Italy, and every time I get this notion to go off the wild end, I picture her praying."

"You've got to be kidding!"

"Nope."

"So, that ruined your trip?"

"Not really. I had a great time, and I have no regrets. What more could a girl ask for?"

"I could think of a couple things."

"Yeah, well, I bet you don't have a granny like mine."

The problem is, not many kids do.

When they come to visit you, let them see your prayer journal and your prayer calendar. Even if they don't have anything to add at the moment, they will have a visual reminder that you are serious about the business of prayer.

If you have a regular prayer time each week (or month) for them, let them know what day of the week and what time during the day you are in prayer.

"It's Tuesday morning, and Grandpa's praying for me."

Don't merely mention that you were praying for them, but share with them what you specifically prayed for, and what you asked God to do about the situation.

"Patrick, I prayed for you last Friday during that tough math test at school. I asked the Lord to allow you to recall all the facts about the math that you've learned and that the test might be an accurate reflection of your true knowledge in the subject."

Throughout the year remind them of your consistent prayers. And when they report to you some result that is an answer to one of your prayers, make sure you give the Lord both private and public gratitude for His graciousness.

Find out what kinds of things they'd like you to be praying about.

Your ability to secure this information will certainly vary from grandchild to grandchild. Some will have a handful of requests (often dealing with material possessions that they simply cannot live without), and others will never have any suggestions.

If they are at your house or around you when you have your prayer journal open, show them their page and then ask, "Is there something you want me to add?"

If they are not around, write a note at least once a year that mentions that you're updating your prayer journal and wondered if they had any special requests.

Keep checking with them year after year even if they never respond to your questions. You want to let them know that your prayers for them will be a consistent, lifetime project. The day may come when they are so broken in spirit that they humbly ask for your prayer support. In the meantime you have established a pattern of true prayer concern.

Share with them your own personal prayer requests.

Whether or not they pray for you will be their decision before the Lord. But when you ask for their prayers on your behalf, you imply several important lessons. They learn things such as:

Grandparents need prayer, too.
You don't have all the answers.

Your Christian life is still growing.
Kids' prayers are important.
We all need each other.

Jot down in a letter that you're worried about the pain in your left arm, and you would appreciate their prayers next Tuesday.

Most kids would appreciate a little help in knowing how to pray, so you might say, in the above case, "Valerie, pray that the doctors will be able to diagnose the problem quickly and find a treatment that will allow me to continue teaching my Sunday school class." Now they know what to ask the Lord.

BIBLICAL ENCOURAGEMENTS TO PRAY

These biblical encouragements to pray aptly fit the life of a praying grandparent:

- Don't lose heart in praying (Luke 18:1-8).
- Pray that your grandchildren won't give in to the many temptations that face them daily (Luke 22:40).
- Remember that even when you aren't sure how to pray for your grandchildren, the Holy Spirit will assist you (Romans 8:26).
- Pray that they do no wrong (2 Corinthians 13:7).
- Pray that they might be made complete, the perfect result of how God intended them to be (2 Corinthians 13:9).
- Pray that your grandchildren's love may grow more and more (Philippians 1:9-10).
- Pray that God might count them worthy of their calling, in order that the name of the Lord Jesus may be glorified in them (2 Thessalonians 1:11-12).
- Pray that their faith may not fail (Luke 22:32).
- Pray that they will have strength to escape all the things that are about to take place (Luke 21:36).
- Always thank God for your grandchildren with real joy in your heart for each memory of them He has allowed you to have (Philippians 1:3-4).

The saints of the Bible took prayer seriously. They did not consider it a luxury for the wealthy or the retired. It was, to them, a solemn duty. To fail to pray was as serious as purposely breaking one of God's commandments.

When Samuel, the aged prophet, priest, and leader of the Hebrew people, decided to retire and allow the new king, Saul, to rule, the people came to him in a multitude and begged him to keep praying for them.

They were afraid that now that he was no longer responsible for the day to day leadership of the land, he would withdraw his prayer support as well.

Samuel's answer is classic.

"Moreover, as for me, far be it from me that I should sin against the Lord by ceasing to pray for you; but I will instruct you in the good and right way" (1 Samuel 12:23).

Even when they are no longer under his care . . . even when they now had another leader . . . even though they might not have a great desire to follow his teaching . . . Samuel would not even think of abandoning his prayer for them.

It was his solemn duty to God to pray for them.

To reject that duty was, for Samuel, sin against the Lord.

Grandkids.

They are not under our control.

They do not always listen to our counsel and advice.

They might seldom, if ever, write or call or visit.

But they are still ours.

There is a solemn duty of prayer to complete.

Far be it from any one of us that we should cease praying for them.

14

How to Be a Grandparent
Your Grandkids Can Count On

We sat in the audience at the small elementary school auditorium and waited for the speaker of the evening. It was quite a rare treat to have a man of such stature visit our rural community. The string of prestigious doctorates that trailed his name in the program shamed the rest of us mortals. He had been president of an eastern university, two terms as a congressman, and now served on a presidential commission.

Toward the back, several reporters from nearby newspapers took practice flashes. After a welcome by the school principal and the pledge of allegiance led by a soft spoken eighth-grade boy, it was time for the introduction of the speaker.

A nine-year-old girl approached the podium. She yanked at the microphone, crackling it down to her level. Then she cleared her throat, which amplified across the room, giggled, and let out a big sigh. The crowd chuckled and also began to relax.

Then she pulled out a small piece of white paper and carefully unfolded it.

With all the dignity allowed a nine-year-old, she took a deep breath and began . . .

"Fellow students . . . teachers and staff . . . parents . . . ladies and gentlemen . . . it gives me a great pleasure to introduce to you . . . "

There was a slight pause, and the perky young lady broke into the world's widest grin.

" . . . MY GRANDPA!"

She grabbed up the paper, spun around on the platform, gave a big hug to the honored guest, and sat down.

The crowd broke into a thunderous ovation. We weren't clapping for the eminent scholar, statesman, and celebrity. We were clapping for this little girl's grandfather.

When the crowd settled down and the man regained his composure, he wiped back an obvious tear and quietly said, "I've never in my life had a better introduction than that."

We're sure he's right.

Can there be any higher acclaim than to see the shine in the eyes and face of a youngster that yells with utter abandonment, "Hi, Grandma! Hi, Grandpa!"

One of the warmest benedictions in Scripture is found in Psalm 128:6, "Indeed, may you see your children's children." It was a powerful motivation in the lives of the ancient Hebrews, and it remains powerful today.

Not only should grandparents be able to get to know their grandchildren, but the reverse is true as well. We've got to be the kind of grandparents our grandkids can count on. We must strive for a level of stability that builds confidence and trust in the next generation and the ones to come.

Many of us are convinced that we need to play an important part in our grandchildren's lives, but we're not sure where to begin. One good thing about being a grandparent is that you can't be fired. You can just muddle along, with no direction or purpose, hoping everything turns out fine. You'll still be called Grandpa . . . and you'll probably still receive another tie for Christmas.

But, for some, that just isn't good enough.

You are determined to do more.

However, a book like this can present so many ideas, you feel overwhelmed.

Here's what we suggest.

Shore Up Your Spiritual Life

No matter where you are in your walk with the Lord, give it a thorough examination. Hold your life up to the mirror of Scripture, and see if you like the reflection.

Paul said a person should not "think more highly of himself than he ought to think; but to think so as to have sound judgment" (Romans 12:3).

So, once again, look at the sin in your life—and confess it. Rebuild some good Bible study habits. Rekindle an active prayer time. Get back into that Bible study group. Try an old-fashioned spring cleaning of your spiritual priorities.

Mend Some Fences

Where are the broken relationships in your family? If they're not broken, are they bent or strained? You will need to work through those rough spots quickly. Then you can get back to the routine of good grandparenting.

Jesus stated a similar principle when He said, "If therefore you are presenting your offering at the altar, and there remember that your brother has something against you, leave your offering there before the altar, and go your way; first be reconciled to your brother, and then come and present your offering" (Matthew 5:23-24).

The Lord is not terribly impressed when we plunge into a program of good relations with one part of the family, while other parts of the family remain at odds with us.

Pick Out One of the Communication Projects

If you are searching for just the right place to begin, how about a project centered around talking to, or writing to, your grandkids more often? We keep saying things like, "I haven't talked to the grandkids in a long time," or, "I know I ought to write to them more often . . . "

Just think, within thirty minutes from now you could be on your way. You can lay down this book and go write that letter or make that phone call.

Not tomorrow.

Not this week.

Not soon.

Now.

Paul once reminded Timothy of his rich heritage when he said, "I am mindful of the sincere faith within you, which first dwelt in your grandmother Lois, and your mother Eunice, and I am sure that it is in you as well" (2 Timothy 1:5).

So, go on . . . write a letter to your little Timmy.

LOOK FOR A WEAK RELATIONSHIP

A good place to begin is the relationship that needs the most help. Maybe you've got a grandson in the service and haven't seen him in years. Maybe there's a granddaughter in Alaska whom you've never seen. Some barrier has come between you and your grandchildren.

Abraham's grandson Jacob tried to live up to his name, "the deceiver" or "trickster." He bartered with his brother, Esau, plotted with his mother, Rebekah, lied to his father, Isaac, and finally had to flee the Promised Land. But he returned years later and raised his large family. When his favorite son, Joseph, was sold off by his brothers, Jacob mourned for years.

But his life didn't end with that sorrow. There was a day when he was finally reunited with Joseph. A day when they fell on each other's neck and wept (Genesis 46:29). And there is no more touching scene:

> When Israel [Jacob] saw Joseph's sons, he said, "Who are these?" And Joseph said to his father, "They are my sons, whom God has given me here." So he said, "Bring them to me, please, that I may bless them." Now the eyes of Israel were so dim from age that he could not see. Then Joseph brought them close to him, and he kissed them and embraced them. And Israel said to Joseph, "I never expected to see your face, and behold, God has let me see your children as well." (Genesis 48:8-11)

Maybe you've got some grandchildren you think you will never see again. Hang in there. Don't give up. Start working from your side of things to re-establish those relationships.

Tackle One Project at a Time

"Wow! I can't do all this!" you complain.

Sure you can.

But you can only do it one step at a time.

You don't have to start all over.

You don't have to try everything immediately.

Don't let past mistakes prevent you from trying something new.

Don't count on past successes allowing you to coast the rest of the way.

Right now would be a good time to flip back through each chapter of this book and review the various topics. As you do that you are going to find that certain sections attract you more than others. You'll be drawn to this idea—or that one. You'll say something like, "I know I really should do something about that."

That's where to begin.

Relax about everything else. Start with one good idea. The others will wait. You can take a look at them next week, or next month, or next year.

Jesus once said, "Therefore you are to be perfect, as your heavenly Father is perfect" (Matthew 5:48).

In a spiritual sense, we are made perfect, in God's eyes, when we accept Christ and are given His righteousness.

But down here on earth, we are not made instantly perfect. So we begin the process of perfection, conforming one area of our life, and then another, to the "measure of the stature which belongs to the fulness of Christ" (Ephesians 4:13).

Some of us will take longer to get there than others, but we are on our way.

One step at a time.

Have Fun

We just came back from the county fair. When you live in a county that has barely four thousand people, the fair is extremely important. We watched, with delight, as county youngsters showed their home-raised animals.

The Intermediate Class of showing and fitting sheep was won by an eleven-year-old friend of ours. She was thrilled to win the big ribbon, and we rejoiced with her. As the judge explained why he selected that particular girl, he concluded with these words, "The only thing I would have liked to have seen different was the girl's expression. It would have been great to see a smile. I like to think the kids are having fun."

So intense in the competition, Hannah had forgotten to smile.

Grandmas and grandpas can be that way too.

We can get so intense with accomplishing what we think are God's goals that we make the whole process a chore. Relationships aren't meant to be that way.

Go back to Proverbs 17:6: "Grandchildren are the crown of old men." The crown. The royalty. The splendor. The very object you want to show off to others.

Good grandparenting is not just a task to be performed out of Christian duty.

Married young, she never finished school. Society would call her unskilled by today's standards. Besides raising a family, she cooked meals for fifty hungry ranch hands. She made her own soap, cranked her own wringer washer, and rolled a pie crust that would melt in your mouth.

Soft spoken, mild mannered, agreeable almost to a fault, we used to think of her as a little naive. But then we realized that at some point in her many years, she deliberately chose to see life that way. She not only hoped and prayed that everything would turn out well, she counted on it.

There was nothing she wouldn't bake for her grandkids. There was nothing in her modest home she wouldn't give to any that even hinted they had need for it. And there was nothing in her mind that they couldn't accomplish. She just knew she had three brilliant grandchildren.

When Granny died, she didn't leave a vast estate. There wasn't much left that she hadn't already given away. Oh, there was a little one bedroom house in the poorer side of town, a thirty-year-old sofa, and some fancy embroidered pillowcases. But not much else.

She did leave her three grandchildren with a lifetime of loving, laughing memories.

Two are now ministers of the gospel, helping others find the Lord. The third is a gifted school teacher and administrator, encouraging little ones to learn.

Granny would be proud.

Plumb proud.

"Of course," you say, "they might have turned out just the same without her gentle influence."

Yep.

They might have.

But we know three grandkids who wouldn't want to find out.

Life can survive without grandparents.

But it's a poorer life indeed.

Remember Proverbs 13:22? "A good man leaves an inheritance to his children's children."

Being the kind of grandparent your grandkids can count on. That's a legacy every grandparent on earth has an equal chance to leave.

Index

Acting like your mate, 42
Acting your age, 140
Active grandparents, 15
Adventuresome spirit, 17

Baby-sitting
    developing a strategy,
        168-70
    no-no's, 170-71
    why kids like it, 164-65
    why parents like it, 162-64
    why some grandparents
        hate it, 165-68
Basic attitudes for good grand-
    fathers, 19
Basic attitudes for good grand-
    mothers, 21
Be Your Mate's Best Friend, 42
Bedtime hours, 99
Behavior, biblical basis for, 144-
    46
Bezalel's spiritual gifts, 90-94
Bigger audience, 13

Blessing your grandchildren, 37
Books, finding the right, 129-30
Bragging rights, 14
Building relationships as a team,
    43

Calendar
    for grandchildren's activi-
        ties, 33
    for prayer, 176
Center stage, when to enter and
    exit, 29
Changing
    habits, 32
    rules, 49
Communicating with modern
    technology, 63
Communication in divorced
    families, 120-21
Communication project, 187-
    88
Complimenting your grand-
    child's mother, 105-6

Conversation conflicts, 101-2
Craftsmanship as a gift of God, 90

Danger of unresolved parenting, 41
Daughter-in-law, asking advice from, 106
Deferring home leadership roles, 107
Demonstrating a spiritual dimension, 16
Devotions, faithful example in, 127-29
Dignified, defined, 20
Disagreement, seven dangerous areas, 97-103
Discipline of grandkids
    accepting secondary responsibility, 138-39
    disagreements, 97-103
    enforcing the rules, 48
    questioning in public, 98
    punishments, 47
    teaching the rules, 49
Distance problem, overcoming the, 54
Divorce and forgiveness, 119
Divorce, listening to both sides, 114-15

Economic priorities that change, 27

Faith, growing, 17
Family
    culture, 11
    history, 71-79

history, enemies of recording, 68-71
    mapping the, 77-78
    security, 12
    tree, how to make a, 71-74
Favoritism, 40
Food and nutrition conflicts, 99-100
Fun, 189-91

Gift-buying conflicts, 101
Gifts, for no reason at all, 35
Gifts, preapproved, 106
Gossip, 142
Gossips, malicious, 22
Grandchildren, expecting the best from, 139-40
Grandmas—different from mothers, 10
Grandparents, imperfect but growing, 146-48
Grandparents were once grandchildren, 26
Grandpas—different from dads, 10

Historical points of interest, 155-56
Holidays as a teaching opportunity, 130-31
Hugging the whole family, 107

Jesus and kids, 167-68
Journal, ten crucial questions, 76-77
Journaling, 74-77

Kid-proof your home, 168

Kids, grandparents as baby-sitters of, 164-65
Know your
    grandkids, 84-85
    limitations to teaching grandkids, 86-88
    skills, business, 85-86
    talents, 83-84

Letter writing
    consistency, 56
    lousy at, 70
    month-by-month ideas, 57-61
Long-range goals, advantage of, 143
Manners, how to teach them, 140
Mending fences, 187
Modeling good behavior, 141-42

Nothing important happens to you? 68-70

Obeying the Word of God, 125
One at a time visits, 153-54

Parents of grandchildren
    divorced, 111-19
    keeping them human, 14
    projects for supporting, 105-7
    public support, 98
    why conflicts with, 103-5
Passive grandparents, 15
Perfect grandparents, 23

Photography for grandparents, 65
Photographs—what you must do now! 78-79
Phrases that spell disaster, 96-97
Power plays, 42
Prayer
    biblical encouragements, 183-84
    calendar, monthly, 176
    guidelines, 177-83
    grandparents who are serious about it, 174-83
    journal, 174-75
    letting them know you are praying, 180-82
    finding out what to pray for, 182
    sharing your own personal requests, 182-83
Prejudice, 142
Projects
    direct involvement in, 106
    for good grandparents, 24
    one at a time, 187-88
Providing life's extras, 14

Reading to your grandchildren, 132
Recipe file for grandkids, 32-33
Reflective grandparents, 60
Remarriage of grandchildren's parents, 119-20
Reverent in behavior, 22
Role, understanding your irreplaceable, 18, 115-16
Role models, 76

Rules for our house, 46
      concerning spiritual mat-
            ters, 46
      dealing with relationships,
            47
      dealing with special condi-
            tions, 47
      general rules, 47
Rules
      that collide, 51
      that work, 50

Second opinion, 13
Self-centeredness, 142
Sense of history, 12
Sensible, defined, 20
Short-range goals, danger of,
      142-43
Solving differences quickly, 42
Sound
      in faith, 20
      in love, 21
      in perseverance, 21
Spiritual family tree, 73
Spiritual life, your own, 125-27
Spiritual teaching and growth
      conflicts, 102-3
Spiritual truth, dos and don'ts,
      125-33
Spoiling, 30-32
Step-grandchildren, 44
Sunday school, taking the
      grandkids to, 129

Tape recordings, 63-64
Teaching
      counting the cost of, 89

      heart for, 93
      what is good, 23
Telephone calls, meaningful,
      62-63
Television conflicts, 100-101
Testimony, tool for teaching,
      128
Time, how much to give to
      each, 34
Traveling with grandkids,
      guidelines, 156-57
"Train up a child. . . ", 31
Treating grandkids different, 31

Vacations, 156-58
      finding the right ones,
            150-51
      what grandkids gain, 158
      what parents gain, 158
      what grandparents gain,
            158
Videos, 64-65
Visits
      activities in your area, 154
      a real vacation, 150-56
      arranging the timing,
            152-53
      eight things to do, 105-7
      focus, 151-52
      one at a time, 153-54
Volunteering
      to baby-sit before you're
            asked, 169
      to help with the party, 106

Weak relationships, 188
"Why, Grandma?" 143-44

Willingness to be misunderstood, 19, 31-32
Wine, enslaved to, 22
Wisdom gained by life near the
finish line, 30

Words and phrases with double
meanings, 107

Yearly survey, 54-56

For information regarding
speaking engagements or seminars
write or call:

Stephen and Janet Bly
Box 157
Winchester, Idaho 83555
(208) 924-5885